25.95

5-09

Gale

OPPOSING
VIEWPOINTS®
SERIES

Outsourcing

Other Books of Related Interest:

Opposing Viewpoints Series
Free Trade

At Issue Series
What Is the Future of the U.S. Economy?

Current Controversies Series
Importing from China

"Congress shall make no law . . . abridging the freedom of speech, or of the press."

First Amendment to the U.S. Constitution

The basic foundation of our democracy is the First Amendment guarantee of freedom of expression. The Opposing Viewpoints Series is dedicated to the concept of this basic freedom and the idea that it is more important to practice it than to enshrine it.

Outsourcing

David M. Haugen, Susan Musser, and Kacy Lovelace,
Book Editors

GREENHAVEN PRESS
A part of Gale, Cengage Learning

GALE
CENGAGE Learning

Detroit • New York • San Francisco • New Haven, Conn • Waterville, Maine • London

GALE
CENGAGE Learning™

Christine Nasso, *Publisher*
Elizabeth Des Chenes, *Managing Editor*

© 2009 Greenhaven Press, a part of Gale, Cengage Learning.

Gale and Greenhaven Press are registered trademarks used herein under license.

For more information, contact:
Greenhaven Press
27500 Drake Rd.
Farmington Hills, MI 48331-3535
Or you can visit our Internet site at gale.cengage.com

For product information and technology assistance, contact us at

Gale Customer Support, 1-800-877-4253
For permission to use material from this text or product, submit all requests online at www.cengage.com/permissions

Further permissions questions can be emailed to permissionrequest@cengage.com

Articles in Greenhaven Press anthologies are often edited for length to meet page requirements. In addition, original titles of these works are changed to clearly present the main thesis and to explicitly indicate the author's opinion. Every effort is made to ensure that Greenhaven Press accurately reflects the original intent of the authors. Every effort has been made to trace the owners of copyrighted material.

Cover photograph reproduced by Brand X Pictures/Punchstock.

LIBRARY OF CONGRESS CATALOGING-IN-PUBLICATION DATA

Outsourcing / David M. Haugen, Susan Musser, and Kacy Lovelace, book editors.
p. cm. -- (Opposing viewpoints)
Includes bibliographical references and index.
ISBN 978-0-7377-4376-0 (hardcover)
ISBN 978-0-7377-4375-3 (pbk.)
1. Contracting out--United States--Juvenile literature I. Haugen, David M., 1969-
II. Musser, Susan. III. Lovelace, Kacy.
HD3861.U6.O93 2009
338.8'7--dc22
2008045341

Printed in the United States of America
1 2 3 4 5 6 7 13 12 11 10 09

Contents

Chapter 3: How Should the Government Regulate Outsourcing?

Chapter 4: What Is the Global Impact of Outsourcing?

Why Consider Opposing Viewpoints?

"The only way in which a human being can make some approach to knowing the whole of a subject is by hearing what can be said about it by persons of every variety of opinion and studying all modes in which it can be looked at by every character of mind. No wise man ever acquired his wisdom in any mode but this."

John Stuart Mill

In our media-intensive culture it is not difficult to find differing opinions. Thousands of newspapers and magazines and dozens of radio and television talk shows resound with differing points of view. The difficulty lies in deciding which opinion to agree with and which "experts" seem the most credible. The more inundated we become with differing opinions and claims, the more essential it is to hone critical reading and thinking skills to evaluate these ideas. Opposing Viewpoints books address this problem directly by presenting stimulating debates that can be used to enhance and teach these skills. The varied opinions contained in each book examine many different aspects of a single issue. While examining these conveniently edited opposing views, readers can develop critical thinking skills such as the ability to compare and contrast authors' credibility, facts, argumentation styles, use of persuasive techniques, and other stylistic tools. In short, the Opposing Viewpoints Series is an ideal way to attain the higher-level thinking and reading skills so essential in a culture of diverse and contradictory opinions.

In addition to providing a tool for critical thinking, Opposing Viewpoints books challenge readers to question their own strongly held opinions and assumptions. Most people form their opinions on the basis of upbringing, peer pressure, and personal, cultural, or professional bias. By reading carefully balanced opposing views, readers must directly confront new ideas as well as the opinions of those with whom they disagree. This is not to simplistically argue that everyone who reads opposing views will—or should—change his or her opinion. Instead, the series enhances readers' understanding of their own views by encouraging confrontation with opposing ideas. Careful examination of others' views can lead to the readers' understanding of the logical inconsistencies in their own opinions, perspective on why they hold an opinion, and the consideration of the possibility that their opinion requires further evaluation.

Evaluating Other Opinions

To ensure that this type of examination occurs, Opposing Viewpoints books present all types of opinions. Prominent spokespeople on different sides of each issue as well as well-known professionals from many disciplines challenge the reader. An additional goal of the series is to provide a forum for other, less known, or even unpopular viewpoints. The opinion of an ordinary person who has had to make the decision to cut off life support from a terminally ill relative, for example, may be just as valuable and provide just as much insight as a medical ethicist's professional opinion. The editors have two additional purposes in including these less known views. One, the editors encourage readers to respect others' opinions—even when not enhanced by professional credibility. It is only by reading or listening to and objectively evaluating others' ideas that one can determine whether they are worthy of consideration. Two, the inclusion of such viewpoints encourages the important critical thinking skill of objectively evaluating an author's credentials and bias. This evaluation will illuminate an author's reasons for taking a particular stance on an issue and will aid in readers' evaluation of the author's ideas.

It is our hope that these books will give readers a deeper understanding of the issues debated and an appreciation of the complexity of even seemingly simple issues when good and honest people disagree. This awareness is particularly important in a democratic society such as ours in which people enter into public debate to determine the common good. Those with whom one disagrees should not be regarded as enemies but rather as people whose views deserve careful examination and may shed light on one's own.

Thomas Jefferson once said that "difference of opinion leads to inquiry, and inquiry to truth." Jefferson, a broadly educated man, argued that "if a nation expects to be ignorant and free ... it expects what never was and never will be." As individuals and as a nation, it is imperative that we consider the opinions of others and examine them with skill and discernment. The Opposing Viewpoints Series is intended to help readers achieve this goal.

David L. Bender and Bruno Leone,
Founders

Introduction

> *"Those who refuse to believe that the developing world is redefining the marketplace are shortsighted, bordering on arrogant. Adding these billions of voices to the global marketplace can't help but reshape the economic order."*
>
> William J. Amelio,
> Business Week Online, June 2, 2008.

> *"Offshore outsourcing can be a great way to cut costs, and it can even improve quality when it forces companies to tighten their internal-development processes. But unless companies spend the time to evaluate all the risks and whether it's a good fit for their individual circumstances, offshore outsourcing can be a lesson in lost time, money, quality, and productivity."*
>
> Mary Hayes Weier,
> Information Week, October 20, 2003.

Although the term outsourcing has commanded media attention in the twenty-first century, the practice of outsourcing has existed in the Unites States for more than a century. During the nation's rapid industrialization in the nineteenth century, most manufacturing companies controlled all aspects of their businesses from design to marketing. Yet at this time, there arose service businesses that catered to specific needs of industries that the industries were willing to forego handling themselves. Private insurance companies, for example, gained industrial clients, and engineering firms were contracted to design and build the offices and factories that dotted the industrial landscape. Still, these service businesses were typically local and carried out functions that did not involve the chain of product manufacturing.

Offshoring, or outsourcing to foreign countries, did not begin in earnest until the mid-twentieth century. At that time, offshoring was limited to relatively cheap items such as toys and clothing because foreign markets such as Japan, China, and India could provide inexpensive labor that made domestic production in the United States a losing proposition. This second wave of outsourcing clearly denoted a trend in industrial manufacture, for now key elements of the manufacturing process were conducted outside the United States.

The third wave of outsourcing followed closely on the heels of the second wave and proved to be a natural extension of that trend. In the 1970s and 1980s, American hi-tech companies were already feeling the effects of competition from Germany and Japan, two nations that exported well-crafted electronics to hungry U.S. consumers. Computer and electronic firms looked to Europe and Asia to find cheaper— sometimes better made—components for the growing U.S. and global markets. Companies were able to keep their outsourcing to a minimum, though, and confine it to specialized products. Thus, the public had little fear of this phenomenon, especially given that media attention focused on the loss of American jobs as automakers and other industries squared off against Japan and a host of global competitors that seemed to be producing cheap, reliable, and desirable consumer goods on vast scales.

In the twenty-first century, outsourcing has moved from the periphery to the mainstream—capturing global markets and public notice. The focus today has shifted from the outsourcing of products to the offshoring of information technology (IT) largely because the Internet revolution has facilitated the transfer of data to any region of the world. While call center support services in India, Canada, and the Czech Republic have perhaps garnered the most attention, drug research and development, payroll processing, accounting, and other services are all part of the $400 billion a year outsourcing boom. Outsourcing has become such a prevalent aspect of American industry—indeed, global industry—that its sheer scope and economic impact simply cannot be ignored.

Proponents of outsourcing believe the system provides several advantages to businesses operating in a global market. Outsourcing allows companies to focus their energies on "core functions"—the heart of their service or manufacturing sectors—while relieving them of ancillary duties. For example, medical providers might outsource billing services in order to devote more personnel and talent to health care. Outsourcing also gives companies the opportunity to lower the costs of in-house infrastructure changes by sending new tasks to out-of-house providers. The business and financial Web site AllBusiness clearly advises small businesses on the benefits of outsourcing. The organization asserts, "Outsourcing converts fixed costs into variable costs, releases capital for investment elsewhere in your business, and allows you to avoid large expenditures in the early stages of your business." AllBusiness informs small business owners that "outsourcing can also make your firm more attractive to investors, since you're able to pump more capital directly into revenue-producing activities."

In a 2006 Hewitt survey of nearly one hundred large U.S. employers, more than half responded that cost-cutting had little or nothing to do with the decision to outsource human resource duties such as payroll and retirement account maintenance. Better performance was the prime motivation, and access to more skilled professionals was another main reason for choosing to outsource. According to many champions of outsourcing, the United States is not producing as many skilled technicians as it once did, and foreign countries such as India are filling needed quotas of trained professionals. Whether such a dearth of talent exists in the United States is debatable, but roughly 60 percent of respondents to the Hewitt survey reported that access to outside talent was a significant reason to outsource human resource tasks.

Even companies that engage in outsourcing, though, are quick to point out that it is not a flawless business solution. Especially with offshored services, some find it difficult to form strong relationships with providers that are not driven by the same goals or that share the same commitments. Others have noted that outsourcing key product or design projects might make in-house staff leave if these aspects of production are the most fulfilling or engaging. In essence, some companies send valuable work to outside vendors and end up losing control of their products. Or as the Web site Offshore IT Outsourcing puts it, "When consultants are running the show, you've reached the dark side of outsourcing."

Some critics ignore the technical and practical stumbling blocks and insist that the dark side of outsourcing involves moral dilemmas. In an article for the *San Diego Union-Tribune*, economics professor Steven M. Mintz asserts that "outsourcing is just another example . . . of putting economic and political interests ahead of doing the right thing." According to Mintz, the rush to lower corporate costs is compromising client confidentiality as personal medical and financial information is transferred overseas for processing in countries like India. In Mintz's view, consumers should be warned and given the ability to opt out of such arrangements if they believe their privacy is threatened.

The fourth wave of outsourcing calls into question IT concerns such as Mintz's, but the trend—though blossoming quickly—is still new enough to be the subject of healthy debate. Outsourcing advocates contend that limiting outsourcing is tantamount to slowing free trade—an inadvisable move for a nation that stands behind globalization. But like Mintz, many detractors believe that America cannot remain an economic giant if its workers must sacrifice jobs for corporate gains. In *Opposing Viewpoints: Outsourcing*, many experts in both camps offer their opinions on the newest wave of outsourcing. In chapters titled "What Is the Impact of Offshore Outsourcing on Americans?" "What Is the Impact of Outsourcing on National Security?" "How Should the Government Regulate Outsourcing?" and "What Is the Global Impact of Outsourcing?" these experts reveal how the fourth wave is shaping the domestic and global economy. For better or worse, outsourcing today is impacting nearly every industry in the United States and the world, and the outcome of this economic trend is likely to determine the future of business and the way in which national economies rise or fall in the global marketplace.

OPPOSING
VIEWPOINTS®
SERIES

CHAPTER 1

What Is the Impact of Offshore Outsourcing on Americans?

Chapter Preface

In the 2004 Economic Report of the President, the George W. Bush administration claimed that America is wise to take advantage of outsourcing opportunities. The report stated that "when a good or service is produced more cheaply abroad, it makes more sense to import it than to make or provide it domestically." Since the issuing of the report, the administration has remained staunch in its defense of corporate outsourcing despite admitting that unsatisfactory consequences have arisen.

In April 2004, N. Gregory Mankiw, chairman of Bush's Council of Economic Advisors and one of the most influential economists in the world, clarified before Congress the administration's view of outsourcing. Mankiw testified,

> The benefits from new forms of trade, such as in services, are no different from the benefits from traditional trade in goods. Outsourcing of professional services is a prominent example of a new type of trade. The gains from trade that take place over the Internet or telephone lines are no different than the gains from trade in physical goods transported by ship or plane. When a good or service is produced at lower cost in another country, it makes sense to import it rather than to produce it domestically. This allows the United States to devote its resources to more productive purposes.

But Mankiw's statement was met with a stony response from Congress. Many members of Congress did not agree that this type of trading, the trading of services, was beneficial to Americans. Because America has lost its manufacturing edge to foreign competitors, several concerned members of Congress believe that the nation must fight to hold on to its service jobs.

During a 2006 trip to New Delhi, India, President Bush continued to promote a new world view in which America's part in a global economy may mean short-term job loss but will include a new surge in training Americans for the professions needed in the future. Bush said, "It's painful for those who lose jobs but the fundamental question is, how does a government or society react to that. And it's basically one of two ways. One is to say, losing jobs is painful, therefore, let's throw up protectionist walls. And the other is to say, losing jobs is painful, so let's make sure people are educated so they can find—fill the jobs of the twenty-first century."

Critics worry, however, that America's young adults are not up to the educational task. The United States graduates a drastically smaller amount of engineers than China or India, and American twelfth-grade students test comparably lower on math and science exams than their peers in those nations. And because China and India are the two main outlets for outsourced American jobs, these critics fear that America may never recover from its comparative lack of skilled professionals.

In the following chapter, Brink Lindsey defends the notion that outsourcing will ultimately benefit the national economy and create new jobs even as old ones move overseas. Economists like Lindsey regret the short-term loss of American jobs but insist that global competition helps hold down labor costs and slow inflation rates in the United States. Other experts in this chapter debate this view, claiming that while outsourcing may be good for corporations, it is depleting much-needed employment and shrinking America's middle class.

| "The world has changed mightily because hundreds of millions of workers . . . have joined the global work force and are eager to take over work long done by Americans." |

Offshore Outsourcing Will Cost Americans Jobs

Steven Greenhouse

In the following viewpoint, Steven Greenhouse contends that American jobs, especially in high-tech sectors such as software engineering and other fields previously immune to outsourcing, are being sent overseas or handed over to foreign workers at a high rate. He claims that outsourcing benefits corporations, but not American workers, because it leads to unemployment and decreased wages for workers whose jobs are not outsourced. Steven Greenhouse has written for the New York Times *since 1995 as the labor and workplace correspondent, and he is author of the book* The Big Squeeze: Tough Times for the American Worker.

As you read, consider the following questions:

1. According to Greenhouse, what do the two *New York Times* articles he cites suggest about the impact of outsourcing on American companies as opposed to the impact on American workers?

2. What does Greenhouse state as the starting salary of American software engineers and that of most Indian software engineers?

3. What are some of the white-collar jobs that the author says are now being done overseas?

The e-mail seemed innocent enough, but something about it worried Myra Bronstein. It instructed her and the 17 other quality-assurance engineers—a fancy term for software testers—to report to the company's boardroom the next morning. *No way that can be good*, she told herself.

At the time, Myra, then 47, was a senior quality-assurance engineer at WatchMark, a company that developed sophisticated software for cell phone companies. She and the other quality-assurance engineers were a dedicated lot. Sometimes they worked 11 or 12 days straight, sometimes up to 18 hours a day, as WatchMark rushed to meet deadlines to get new software to customers. WatchMark, based in Bellevue, a Seattle suburb, made software that helped wireless companies determine whether their cell towers were working properly and how many calls were being dropped.

Myra remembers one episode when, after being required to work 24 hours in a row testing software, she told her boss that she had to leave for a long-scheduled doctor's appointment. Her boss yelled at her, accusing her of lacking dedication.

"If they wanted to wreck our weekends or cancel our vacations," Myra says, "they'd basically say, 'This is a very important release. We need to build this customer's confidence. We have to show them it's good quality, and we need you to work, and basically if we lose this customer we could fold.' They'd say, 'As long as we're in business, you have a job, so it's in your best interest to work as hard as you can—weekends, evenings, everything.'"

Americans Are Forced to Train Their Replacements

Myra is a petite woman, deliberate and not at all showy. She has a reserved smile, a pale, almond-shaped face, deep-set eyes, and thick, dark hair that just touches her shoulders. As Myra and other quality-assurance engineers gathered in the boardroom the morning after the e-mail arrived, the director of human resources began giving out large manila envelopes. Once everyone was there, Myra recalls, "The head of HR said, 'Unfortunately, we're having layoffs, and you're in the room because you're being impacted by the layoffs.'"

The 18 engineers were dumbstruck, but the head of human services pressed on. "Your replacements," she continued, "are flying in from India, and you're expected to train them if you are going to receive severance."

"People were trying not to cry," Myra says. "We felt sucker-punched. It totally knocked the wind out of me. I had bought into all their motivational tactics. I felt if I helped my company stay afloat, I would ensure my own employment. I believed them."

Uncomfortably, reluctantly, Myra and the others agreed to WatchMark's request to train their replacements beginning the following Monday. They would train their replacements for four to eight weeks and would then receive two months' severance pay. Not to agree would have meant working just a few more days and not receiving any severance.

The following Monday morning, the American engineers gathered inside a conference room, waiting to meet the 20 engineers who had been flown in from India. WatchMark's di-

rector of quality assurance began that meeting ever so clum-
sily by saying, "I'd like my new team to meet my old team."

Once each quality-assurance engineer was assigned an Indian to train—Myra was assigned two—WatchMark's vice
president of technology began a pep talk, telling the laid-off
engineers, "The future welfare of WatchMark depends on how
well you train these people."

For the next two months, Myra strained to maintain her
composure as she trained two Indians at once. "They didn't
acknowledge what was going on, that we had to do something
upsetting," she says. "It was the most difficult situation in the
world."

Soon, Myra and the other Americans began calling themselves "The Castaways" and "Dead Man Working." She was
told that the Indians would earn $5,000 a year; she had earned
$80,000.

High-Tech Was Not America's Salvation

The rise of high-tech, some experts predicted, was to be the
salvation for America's economic ills and beleaguered workers.
And in the late 1990s, the high-tech boom did in fact do won-
ders for the economy, helping to reduce the jobless rate to its
lowest level in decades to lift real wages at their fastest clip in
recent memory. But the high-tech bubble burst in 2000, and
now it seems that if high-tech is going to be a salvation for
anyone, it will be for workers in Bangalore and Beijing.

"Profits, Not Jobs, on the Rebound in Silicon Valley," read
the headline of a *New York Times* story in the summer of
2005. Profits at Silicon Valley's [name given to the region in
Northern California known for its high concentration of high-
tech businesses] seven largest companies had more than quin-
tupled the three previous years, while employment in the valley had declined by nearly 20,000 during the same period. In
contrast, during the high-tech boom from 1995 to 1997, Silicon Valley added more than 82,000 jobs. The *Times* story fo-

cused on Wyse Technology, a respected producer of computer terminals, whose sales and profits were soaring and whose job growth was taking place overseas. In 2005, Wyse added 100 workers in India and 35 in China, increasing its worldwide work force to 380, but Wyse's employment in California remained flat. Just 15 percent of Wyse's engineering talent remained in America.

Another *Times* story that summer was headlined, "Cutting Here, but Hiring Over There." The story began, "Even as it proceeds with layoffs of up to 13,000 workers in Europe and the United States, IBM [International Business Machines Corporation] plans to increase its payroll in India this year by more than 14,000 workers."

These news stories point to a growing disconnect between what's good for American corporations and what's good for American workers. These stories also demonstrate that high-tech will not be a salvation for many American job seekers in the future unless the United States develops some revolutionary new technologies that spawn large new industries.

When factory jobs were heading overseas in the 1980s, young Americans were told there would he plenty of high-paying high-tech jobs to replace the jobs that disappeared. Then in the early 1990s, many companies moved their computer-chip production overseas, and we were told the good software jobs would remain in America. Now many of those software jobs are moving overseas, fueled by some stark numbers. American software engineers start at $75,000 a year, while many in India start at $15,000.

One respected consulting firm, Forrester Research, estimates that 3.4 million white-collar jobs will be sent offshore between 2003 and 2015. Tax returns once prepared by accountants in New York or Los Angeles are now being prepared in the Philippines. Radiologists in India are reviewing X-rays e-mailed from the United States. Paralegals in India are helping budget-minded law firms in Chicago and Seattle prepare

"We're going to have to let you go . . . We've found someone in China who is 45% better at being you for 24% less." Cartoon by Fran. www.CartoonStock.com.

wills and contracts. Forrester Research estimates that from 2003 to 2015, the offshoring exodus will include 542,000 computer jobs, 259,000 management jobs, 191,000 architectural jobs, 79,000 legal jobs, and 1.6 million back-office jobs.

Offshoring's Impact on the Economy

Offshoring may produce other perils as well. Joseph Stiglitz, a Nobel Prize-winning economist and professor at Columbia University, says, "What worries me is that [offshoring] could have an enormous effect on wages, and that could have a wrenching impact on society." Offshoring has already held down wages of software workers up and down the West Coast. At a Sprint call center in North Carolina, 180 customer-service representatives, scared that their jobs would be shipped abroad, accepted a pay freeze for 2004 and no definite increase in 2005.

Three Harvard economists—George J. Borjas, Richard B. Freeman, and Lawrence F. Katz—found that for every 1 percent that employment falls in a manufacturing industry because of imports or operations moving overseas, wages are depressed by five-tenths of 1 percent for the workers who remain. With Forrester Research predicting that 6 percent of service-sector jobs will be sent offshore by 2015, Katz estimates that wages for service-sector workers in vulnerable fields could be shaved by 2 percent to 3 percent as a result. "White-collar workers have a right to be scared," Katz says.

Paul Samuelson, the famed Massachusetts Institute of Technology economist, textbook writer, and Nobel Prize winner, has warned that if American companies shift too many high-tech jobs and too much high-tech expertise to India, China, and other developing nations, that could ultimately undercut American industry and reduce the nation's per capita income. Samuelson also warns of a downward effect on worker pay, saying, "If you don't believe that [offshoring] changes the average wages in America, then you believe in the tooth fairy."

Indeed, more and more economists are voicing fears that if American technology companies continue to send so much of their work and expertise overseas, that might someday enable India's and China's high-tech industries to outinvent, out-think, and outstrip America's high-tech industry in some key areas, leaving the United States at a costly disadvantage in a field of critical importance.

Feeling Forsaken

After two months of training her replacement, Myra was unemployed. That was the last thing she would have anticipated when, full of lofty expectations, she quit her job as a health inspector in Kansas City to pursue a degree in electrical engineering. She hungered for a job that promised more excitement, more money, and more mobility. "At the time, computer science fit all those criteria," she says.

After obtaining her engineering degree, she landed a job with AT&T in Naperville, Illinois, testing its electronic switching systems. Four years after Myra began, AT&T started downsizing in Naperville, so she transferred to AT&T's operation in Middletown, New Jersey. For her first four years there, she wrote user manuals about telephone systems, and then she transferred into software testing. There, Myra was surprised by how many young engineers from India were brought in on H-1B [nonimmigrant] visas. After four years, she was the only Caucasian left in the 20-person testing unit. "The writing was on the wall," Myra said.

Worried that she would be replaced, Myra quit and moved to Seattle, a city for which she long had a romantic hankering. There she took the testing job with WatchMark, and three years later came the abrupt layoffs. Myra remained unemployed for three months before settling for a job at what she called "a testing sweatshop." It paid $20 an hour, half the rate she earned at WatchMark (which has since changed its name to Vallent and been acquired by IBM). Myra's new testing company was across the street from a sewage treatment plant, and in the summer, the workers complained that they were choking from the smell, the heat, and the lack of ventilation. In winters, there was so little heat that many workers wore their coats all day.

"One day it was raining a lot, and I was sitting there at my PC, testing software for bugs, and it started dripping from the ceiling, right into my PC. Before I had time to react, it exploded. Smoke was coming out of it. That was some bug all right."

She soon quit.

Seeing so many jobs being offshored to India, Myra grew convinced that it would be hard to find a high-tech job that paid nearly as much as her WatchMark job. She searched in vain for several more months, supporting herself by drawing down her 401(k) [retirement plan] and selling off her beloved, painstakingly assembled collection of antique Guilloche cosmetic compacts—fine French-made enamel compacts, some of which had silver handles.

Feeling forsaken by the high-tech world, Myra moved back to Kansas City, in large part to take care of her ailing 86-year-old mother.

"I'm giving up on the technology field, because it's so difficult to survive now that employers can use so much cheap, skilled labor overseas," she says.

Myra is now contemplating a radical career change. She is thinking of becoming a pharmacist, which would entail six years of school. But she has no idea how she would afford the tuition. The Trade Adjustment Assistance Act pays tuition for factory workers who lose their jobs to globalization, but Myra was a software worker, not a factory worker.

"I would never have gone into the technology field in the first place if I had a crystal ball and knew the bottom was going to drop out," Myra said. "People who are staying in this field have to go back to school and continually learn more complicated high-tech things. I thought I could be very competent and learn what I needed to know about my own job and serve the company well. But now they want much more from you for much less."

A Bleak Future for American Workers

In today's brave new world of offshoring, no one seems sure where to run for safety. Getting a college degree, especially a degree in computer engineering, used to be the ticket to job security. But as Harvard's Richard Freeman has pointed out, the world has changed mightily because hundreds of millions of workers in India and China, not to mention in Russia, Hungary, and other Soviet Bloc countries, have joined the global work force and are eager to take over work long done by Americans—including highly educated Americans. This has made it hard to advise American college students about what careers to prepare for.

In a candid moment Craig Barrett, chairman of Intel, a company that does research and manufacturing in many different nations, voiced concern that globalization will portend a dimmer future for young Americans: "Intel will be okay no matter what," Barrett said. "We can adjust our R&D [research and development] and manufacturing wherever it is most economically advantageous to do so. But in addition to being chairman of Intel, I am also a grandfather, and I wonder what my grandchildren are going to do."

"*While job losses are real and sometimes very painful, it is important . . . to distinguish between the painful aspects of progress and outright decline.*"

Offshore Outsourcing Will Not Cost Americans Jobs

Brink Lindsey

In the following viewpoint, Brink Lindsey argues that outsourcing is not costing Americans jobs and that the American economy is dynamic, resulting in a constantly fluctuating rate of employment. Lindsey contends that outsourcing will in fact produce more and better jobs for Americans. Brink Lindsey is the director of the Cato Institute's Center for Trade Policy Studies and author of the book Against the Dead Hand: The Uncertain Struggle for Global Capitalism.

As you read, consider the following questions:

1. According to the U.S. Department of Labor's Bureau of Labor Statistics, how many jobs were created and how many were lost between 1993 and 2002?

Brink Lindsey, "Job Losses and Trade: A Reality Check," *Center for Trade Policy Studies Briefing Paper*, March 17, 2004. Republished with permission of The Cato Institute, conveyed through Copyright Clearance Center, Inc.

2. How does outsourcing create new jobs in the United States, according to Lindsey?

3. With what previous job-eliminating phenomenon does Lindsey equate outsourcing?

Is globalization sending the best American jobs overseas? That question has been at the center of trade policy debates for decades now. In the 1980s, setbacks for major industries at the hands of Japanese competition led to claims that the U.S. economy was undergoing "deindustrialization." In the 1990s, [business leader and presidential candidate] Ross Perot famously predicted that the North American Free Trade Agreement [NAFTA] would result in a "giant sucking sound" as jobs went south; later in the decade, market critics warned of a "race to the bottom" in which U.S. multinational corporations moved jobs to wherever wages were lowest and environmental regulations were most lax.

In the past couple of years, the recession and subsequent sluggish recovery have stoked anxieties about job security generally—and, in particular, the threat to job security posed by intensifying foreign competition. Today China and India have replaced Japan and Mexico as the most feared foreign threats to U.S. employment. The world's two most populous countries are supposedly combining to land a one-two punch on American workers: manufacturing jobs are fleeing to China while service-sector jobs are being "offshored" to India.

This [viewpoint] responds to fears about trade-related job losses—and the demagoguery [emotional politics] that exploits those fears—by putting the issue into proper context. Facts and figures presented here demonstrate that trade is only one element in a much bigger picture of incessant turnover in the U.S. job market. Furthermore, these data make clear that the overall trend in that market is toward more and better jobs for American workers. While job losses are real and sometimes very painful, it is important—indeed, for the formulation of sound public policy, it is vital—to distinguish between the painful aspects of progress and outright decline. . . .

The American Economy Is Dynamic

The total number of jobs in the U.S. economy is first and foremost a function of the size of the labor force. As the population grows, the number of people in the work force grows; as the labor supply increases, market forces absorb that supply and deploy labor among different sectors of the economy.

Consider all the major events that increased the supply of labor over the past half century . . . the baby boom, the surge in work force participation by women, and rising rates of immigration after decades of restrictionist policies. Consider as well the key developments that slashed demand for certain kinds of labor: the growing competitiveness of foreign producers and falling U.S. barriers to imports; the move by U.S. companies toward globally integrated production operations and the consequent relocation of many operations overseas; the deregulation of the transportation, energy, and telecommunications industries and the wrenching restructuring that followed; and, most important, wave after wave of labor-saving technological innovation, from containerization that replaced longshoremen to dial phones that replaced switchboard operators to factory-floor robots that replaced assembly-line workers to computers that replaced back-office clerks to automatic teller machines that replaced bank tellers to voice mail that replaced receptionists.

Yet in the face of all this flux, no chronic shortage of jobs ever materialized. Over those tumultuous five decades, a growing economy and functioning labor markets were all that was needed to accommodate huge shifts in labor supply and demand. Now and in the future, sound macroeconomic policies and continued flexibility in labor markets will suffice to generate increasing employment, notwithstanding the rise of China and India and the ongoing advance of digitization.

The Types of Jobs Available Are Constantly Changing

The steady increase in total employment ... masks the frenetic dynamism of the U.S. labor market.... Large numbers of jobs are being shed constantly, even in good times; total employment continues to increase only because even larger numbers of jobs are being created.

The extent of normal job churn is revealed by the weekly statistics on new claims for unemployment insurance. According to economist Brad DeLong, a weekly figure of 360,000 new claims is roughly consistent with a stable unemployment rate. In other words, when the unemployment rate holds steady—that is, total employment grows fast enough to absorb the ongoing increase in the labor force—some 18.7 million people will lose their jobs and file unemployment insurance claims over the course of a year. Meanwhile, even more people will get new jobs....

According to data compiled by the U.S. Department Labor's Bureau of Labor Statistics, total U.S. private-sector employment rose by 17.8 million during the decade from 1993 to 2002. To produce that healthy net increase, a breathtaking total of 327.7 million jobs were added, while 309.9 million jobs were lost. In other words, for every one new net private-sector job created during that period, 18.4 gross job additions had to offset 17.4 gross job losses.

In light of those facts, it is impossible to give credence to claims that job losses in this or that sector constitute a looming catastrophe for the U.S. economy as a whole. Of course, particular industries may encounter difficulties, and involuntary unemployment is always difficult for the individuals and families subjected to it. In the enormous and dynamic U.S. economy, however, it is as inevitable that some companies and industries will shrink as it is that others will expand. Local challenges and problems should not be confused with national crises.

The ongoing growth in total employment is frequently dismissed on the ground that most of the new positions being created are low-paying, dead-end "McJobs." The facts, however, show otherwise.

Management and professional specialty jobs have grown rapidly during the recent era of globalization. Between 1983 and 2002, the total number of such positions climbed from 23.6 million to 42.5 million—an 80 percent increase. In other words, these challenging, high-paying positions have jumped from 23.4 percent of total employment to 31.1 percent.

These high-quality jobs will continue growing in the years to come. According to projections for 2002–12 prepared by the Bureau of Labor Statistics, management, business, financial, and professional positions will grow from 43.2 million to 52.0 million—a 20 percent increase that will lift these jobs from 30.0 percent of total employment to 31.5 percent. . . .

Loss of High-Tech Jobs Exaggerated

Fears about vanishing manufacturing jobs have figured prominently in trade policy debates for decades. . . . Those fears have been compounded by growing anxiety about trade-related jobs losses in the service sector. Advances in information and communications technologies now make it possible for many jobs—ranging from more routine clerical jobs like processing insurance claims and handling customer calls to positions in highly skilled occupations like software development and radiology—to be performed anywhere, with the work then transmitted electronically wherever it is needed.

In particular, the offshoring of information technology (IT) jobs to India and other low-wage countries has received a flurry of recent attention. According to a survey of hiring managers conducted by the Information Technology Association of America, 12 percent of IT companies have already out-sourced some operations to foreign countries. As for future trends, Forester Research has predicted in a widely cited study that 3.3 million white-collar jobs—including 1.7 million back-office positions and 473,000 IT jobs—will move overseas between 2000 and 2015.

Employment in IT-related occupations has experienced a significant decline recently. In 2002, the total number of IT-related jobs stood at 5.95 million—down from the 2000 peak of 6.47 million. Although some of those jobs were lost because of offshoring, the major culprits were the slowdown in demand for IT services after the Y2K [the turn of the millennium] buildup, followed by the dot-com collapse and the broader recession. Moreover, it should be remembered that the recent drop in employment has occurred after a dramatic buildup. In 1994, 1.19 million people were employed as mathematical and computer scientists; by 2000, that figure had jumped to 2.07 million—a 74 percent increase. As of 2002, the figure stood at 2.03 million—still 71 percent higher than in 1994.

Despite the trend toward offshoring, IT-related employment is expected to see healthy increases in the years to come. According to Department of Labor projections, the total number of computer and mathematical occupations will jump from 3.02 million in 2002 to 4.07 million in 2012—a 35 percent increase over the decade. Of the 30 specific occupations projected to grow fastest during the decade, 7 are computer related. Thus, the recent downturn in IT-related employment is likely only a temporary break in a larger trend of robust job growth.

The wild claims that offshoring will gut employment in the IT sector are totally at odds with reality. The IT job losses projected by Forester amount to fewer than 32,000 per year—relatively modest attrition in the context of total IT-related employment of nearly 6 million. These job losses, meanwhile, will be offset by new IT-related jobs as computer and mathematical occupations continue to boom. The doomsayers are thus confusing a cyclical downturn with a permanent trend.

Outsourcing Promotes Growth

Offshoring of IT services to India and elsewhere has been made possible by ongoing advances in computer and communications technologies. If those advances pose a threat to U.S.-based IT services industries, it should be possible to trace the emergence of that threat in trade statistics, since offshoring registers as an increase in services imports.

Yet the fact is that the United States runs a trade surplus in the IT services most directly affected by offshoring. In the categories of "computer and data processing services" and "data base and other information services," U.S. exports rose from $2.4 billion in 1995 to $5.4 billion in 2002, while imports increased from $0.3 billion to $1.2 billion over the same period. Thus, the U.S. trade surplus in these services has expanded from $2.1 billion to $4.2 billion.

Meanwhile, the same technological advances that give rise to offshoring facilitate the international provision of all kinds of services—banking, accounting, legal assistance, engineering, telemedicine, and so on. The United States is a major exporter of services generally and runs a sizable trade surplus. In 2002, for example, services exports accounted for 30 percent of total U.S. exports, and exports exceeded imports by $64.8 billion. Accordingly, the increasing ability to provide services remotely is a commercial boon to many U.S.-based service industries. Although some jobs are doubtless at risk, the same trends that make offshoring possible are creating new oppurtunities—and new jobs—throughout the U.S. economy.

Although offshoring does eliminate jobs, it also yields important benefits. To the extent that companies can reduce costs by shifting certain operations overseas, they are increasing productivity. The process of competition ultimately passes the resulting cost savings on to consumers, which then spurs demand for other goods and services. Thus do productivity increases—whether caused by the introduction of new technology or new ways to organize work—translate into economic growth and rising overall living standards.

In particular, offshoring facilitates the diffusion of IT throughout the U.S. economy. According to Catherine Mann at the Institute for International Economics, globalized production of IT hardware—that is, the offshoring of computer-related manufacturing—accounted for 10 to 30 percent of the drop in hardware prices. The resulting increase in productivity encouraged the rapid spread of computer use and thereby added some $230 billion in cumulative additional GDP [gross domestic product] between 1995 and 2002.

Offshoring offers the potential to take a similar bite out of IT software and services prices. The resulting price falls will promote the further spread of IT—and new business processes that take advantage of cheap IT. As Mann notes, health services and construction are two large and important sectors that today feature low IT intensity (as measured by IT equipment per worker) and below-average productivity growth. Diffusion of IT into these and other sectors could prompt a new round of productivity growth such as that provoked by the globalization of hardware production during the 1990s.

Technology Eliminates Jobs

The attention now being paid to offshoring creates the impression that it is an utterly unprecedented phenomenon. The fact is, though, that the very same technological advances that are making offshoring possible have been eliminating large numbers of white-collar jobs for many years now.

The diffusion of IT throughout the U.S. economy has caused major shakeups in the job market over the past decade. Bank tellers have been replaced by automatic teller machines; receptionists and operators have been replaced by

Outforcing Is the Real Threat

America has long benefited from "insourcing" and "brain gain" in which talented foreigners come to our shores to escape the stifling environment of their homelands. But as other nations adopt market reform, they become friendlier to entrepreneurs and make inroads into what has traditionally been an American advantage. (For example, it was regulatory reform in India in the early 1990s that prompted many multinational corporations to set up operations there.)...

Outforcing persists, to a large degree, because policy makers have been slow to address growing problems. Too often American policy seems to operate on the basis of decades-old assumptions about our nation's place in the world, such as [the following]:

- The United States is the best place to find educated workers.

- U.S. policy provides the best environment for job creation.

- Other Western democracies have rigid economies that are unfriendly to entrepreneurs....

As other nations continue to embrace reform, legislators at every level of government should work to improve our nation's innovation-friendliness to ensure our reputation matches reality. Legislators must see the world as it exists today, and not base policy on outdated assumptions. The same policies that guard against outforcing will also encourage more insourcing.

Ted Balaker and Adrian T. Moore,
"Offshoring and Public Fear: Assessing the Real Threat to Jobs,"
Reason Foundation Policy Study no. 333, May 2005.

voice mail and automated call menus; back-office record-keeping and other clerical jobs have been replaced by computers; layers of middle management have been replaced by better internal communications systems. In all of these cases, jobs are not simply being transferred overseas; they are being consigned to oblivion by automation and the resulting reorganization of work processes.

The increased churn in white-collar jobs can be seen in the Department of Labor's statistics on displaced long-tenured workers, defined as workers who have lost jobs that they held for three years or more. Unsurprisingly, job displacement climbs during recessions and drops during expansions, yet the pattern of displacement has changed markedly over the past couple of decades.

During the severe 1981–82 recession, blue-collar workers were especially hard hit. Some 58 percent of displaced workers had been previously employed in blue-collar occupations, and the displacement rate for such workers stood at 7.3 percent. By contrast, white-collar workers were much less affected by the economic downturn: about one-third of displaced workers had previously held white-collar positions, and the displacement rate was a modest 2.6 percent.

The situation looked very different during the 1991–92 recession. White-collar workers bore more of the brunt of the downturn: more than half of all displaced workers had previously held white-collar jobs, and the displacement rate for those occupations had increased to 3.7 percent. Moreover, displacement rates for white-collar workers stayed relatively high even after the recession ended: the rate was 3.3 percent during 1993–94 and 2.9 percent during 1995–96. In other words, the rate of job loss for long-tenured white-collar workers was higher as the economic boom of the 1990s was getting under way than it had been during the harsh recession of the early 1980s.

Thus, well before the recent flap over offshoring, the digital revolution was rendering some white-collar jobs obsolete—while making possible the creation of other jobs. Offshoring is merely the latest manifestation of a well-established process. The only difference is that, with offshoring, IT is facilitating the transfer of jobs overseas rather than substituting directly for those jobs. In either case, U.S. jobs are lost—the inevitable downside of technological progress and rising productivity. Why is this downside taken in stride when jobs are eliminated entirely yet considered unbearable when the jobs are taken up as hand-me-downs by Indians and other foreigners? . . .

Embracing Change

In recent years, many Americans have lost their jobs and suffered hardship as a result. Many more have worried that their jobs would be next. There is no point in denying these hard realities, but just as surely there is no point in blowing them out of proportion. The U.S. economy is not running out of good jobs; it is merely coming out of a recession. And regardless of whether economic times are good or bad, some amount of job turnover is an inescapable fact of life in a dynamic market economy. This fact cannot be wished away by blaming foreigners; it cannot be undone with trade restrictions.

Public policy can lessen the pain of economic change. It can ease workers' transitions from one job to another; it can produce better educated and better trained workers who are capable of filling higher-paying, more challenging positions; it can promote sound growth and avoid, or at least minimize, economy-wide slumps. But there is no place for policies that seek to stifle change in the name of preserving existing jobs. The innovation and productivity increases that render some jobs obsolete are also the source of new wealth and rising living standards. Embracing change and its unavoidable disruptions is the only way to secure the continuing gains of economic advancement.

"If the United States, its companies and its workers are to remain leaders in the global economy, offshoring must remain a tool available to our corporations."

Offshore Outsourcing Has Many Economic Benefits

Daniel T. Griswold and Dale D. Buss

Daniel T. Griswold and Dale D. Buss argue in the following viewpoint that outsourcing helps the American economy. According to the authors, America is still the world's top provider of outsourcing services and a leader in foreign investment, boosting American job growth as more foreign dollars take advantage of America's opportunities. Griswold and Buss warn that restrictions on outsourcing may alter foreign investment strategies and tarnish America's global image. Daniel T. Griswold serves as the director of the Center for Trade Policy Studies at the Cato Institute and has written extensively on outsourcing and other trade issues. Dale D. Buss is an adjunct scholar at the Mackinac Center, a research and educational center based in Midland, Michigan.

Daniel T. Griswold and Dale D. Buss, "Outsourcing Benefits Michigan Economy and Taxpayers," *Mackinac Center for Public Policy Brief*, September 16, 2004. Reproduced by permission.

As you read, consider the following questions:

1. What are some of the benefits of outsourcing for the U.S. economy cited by the authors?
2. According to the authors, how does outsourcing improve the United States' relationship with India?
3. The authors state that government restrictions on outsourcing could harm the U.S. economy in what four ways?

Lawmakers in Congress and in more than 30 state legislatures have targeted foreign outsourcing as a threat to U.S. employment and prosperity. Along with certain critics in the news media, such as CNN's Lou Dobbs [host of the show *Outsourcing America*], they charge that U.S. companies are firing American workers in significant numbers and replacing them with foreign service workers in low-wage countries such as India. Legislative proposals in Michigan and elsewhere have focused on barring federal or state contracts with companies that would "offshore" the work to call centers or information technology providers abroad.

Foreign outsourcing has become a lightning rod for controversy. At a press conference in February [2004], the chairman of President [George W.] Bush's Council of Economic Advisors, Professor Gregory Mankiw of Harvard, found out just how controversial outsourcing has become. The president's economic advisor described foreign outsourcing as "something that we should realize is probably a plus for the economy in the long run." Far from being a new and unique threat to employment, he noted, "Outsourcing is just a new way of doing international trade. We're very used to goods being produced abroad and being shipped here on ships or planes. What we're not used to is services being produced abroad and being sent here over the Internet or telephone wires." Mankiw concluded, "I don't think [foreign outsourcing] is the primary thing driving the recent business cycle developments." Republican and Democratic politicians alike criticized Mankiw for favoring "economic theory" over displaced workers.

Guilty of Understanding the Benefits

Despite the criticism, the president's chief economic advisor was right. Outsourcing itself is nothing new. U.S. companies and governments have been outsourcing domestically for decades by contracting out such services as payroll, database management, and janitorial services. The new twist has been the recent increase in foreign outsourcing, or offshoring, in which companies buy services from foreign-based providers. Foreign outsourcing has been made increasingly cost-effective because of the personal computer, which has digitized much of our work, and high-speed and deregulated transmission of that information through broadband and the Internet. Informational technology (IT) companies are increasingly outsourcing routine programming, data entry, and system monitoring. Call centers are shifting more of those thankless jobs abroad.

If anything, Mankiw was guilty of understating the benefits of outsourcing. Foreign outsourcing almost certainly benefits the U.S. economy in the short run as well as the long run. Like more conventional forms of trade, foreign outsourcing allows U.S. companies to dramatically cut the cost of certain information technology services. As a result, U.S. companies become more competitive in what they do best, their "core competencies." Better and more affordable services become available for consumers and taxpayers. Outsourcing allows companies to operate on an around-the-clock, "24/7" production cycle, further adding to productivity. Outsourcing is even making possible work that simply wouldn't exist otherwise, such as chasing down delinquent accounts receivable that were thought to be beyond collection.

According to a 2003 study by the McKinsey Global Institute, outsourcing delivers large and measurable benefits to the

U.S. economy. It reduces costs for IT and other services by as much as 60 percent, keeping U.S. companies competitive in global markets, benefiting workers and shareholders alike. It stokes demand abroad for the export of U.S.-supplied computers, telecommunications hardware, software, and legal, financial, and marketing services. It returns profits to the United States from U.S.-owned affiliates abroad, and it allows U.S. companies to re-deploy workers in more productive jobs here at home. In fact, McKinsey calculates that every $1.00 spent on foreign outsourcing creates $1.12 to $1.14 of additional economic activity in the U.S. economy. Another study by Global Insights [an economic and financial analysis organization] estimated the U.S. economy will be $124 billion larger in 2008 if outsourcing continues compared to no outsourcing.

Foreign outsourcing could eventually deliver the same scale of productivity gains to the IT services industry that it has to the hardware industry. Many of the components in a typical computer sold in the United States today are sourced from around the world, especially East Asia. According to a study by [economics professor] Catherine Mann at the Institute for International Economics in Washington, global sourcing for IT hardware cut the final costs to businesses and consumers by 10 to 30 percent, accelerating the diffusion of computer technology through the U.S. economy. That diffusion added three-tenths of a point to GDP [gross domestic product] growth and a cumulative $230 billion to U.S. gross domestic product. Foreign outsourcing, by spreading lower IT costs to service sectors that make up 80 percent of the U.S. economy, could have an even bigger impact on growth than the outsourcing of IT hardware. Outsourcing could help control spiraling costs in such sectors as health care and education. . . .

Outsourcing and Insourcing

Another reality lost in the outsourcing debate is the amount of work the rest of the world outsources to the United States.

We are far and away the world's top "provider" of outsourcing in the form of information technology, financial, communications, and other business services. In 2003, Americans sold $131 billion in private business services to the rest of the world. Those services include such outsourcing tasks as legal work, computer programming, management consulting, telecommunications, banking, and engineering. At the same time, Americans were buying, or importing, $77 billion worth of business services from the rest of the world, including call center and data entry services from developing countries such as India and the Philippines. In other words, when it comes to outsourcing of business services, the United States ran a $54 billion surplus with the rest of the world [in 2003]. As a *Wall Street Journal* report concluded, "The numbers suggest that congressional efforts to restrict outsourcing by U.S. companies may backfire, if they provoke retaliation by U.S. trading partners. Economists also say that U.S. service exporters—insurers, for instance—might lose some competitive edge if they can't use foreign suppliers for call centers or other back-office operations."

In the more specialized area of IT services, America's edge is even more pronounced. In 2002, according to the most recent figures, U.S. companies exported $14.8 billion worth of computer, data processing, research, development, construction, architectural, engineering and other IT services. During that same year, Americans imported $3.9 billion of those same kinds of services. So for every dollar Americans sent abroad for IT outsourcing in 2002, the world sent more than three dollars to the United States for "insourcing."

Foreign Direct Investment Boosts Economy

The same general story applies to foreign direct investment. The United States remains a magnet for direct investment from foreign multinational companies. In 2003, the rest of the world invested $82 billion in directly owned U.S. assets, including foreign-owned affiliates. According to the Commerce Department, more than 6 million Americans work for foreign-owned affiliates in the United States. It is fundamentally misleading to complain about U.S. companies investing abroad without considering foreign investment in the United States. Indeed, if Congress and state legislatures declare war against foreign outsourcing, American companies and workers will be among the first casualties.

Many of those casualties could come specifically in Michigan. The state has gained just as the nation has from direct foreign investment, particularly—and not surprisingly—that clustered around the auto industry. In the '80s, for example, Mazda Motor Corp. built a brand new automotive assembly plant in Flat Rock, Michigan, which still employs several hundred people in well-paid, [United Auto Workers] UAW-represented jobs. Dozens of foreign-owned automotive manufacturers and suppliers have opened technical, sales, marketing and distribution centers as well in the metropolitan area, helping to a significant extent Detroit's continuing efforts to remain the world automotive capital.

Japanese auto makers alone employ thousands of Michiganders in their technical centers. Nissan Motor Co., for example, employs about 800 people at its technical center in Farmington Hills, Michigan. South Korean auto maker Hyundai is to employ nearly 100 people at its new tech center near Ann Arbor, Michigan. Suzuki Motor Corp. has opened a development nexus in Wixom, Michigan, and Mitsubishi Heavy Industries located one in Sterling Heights, Michigan. Toyota Motor Co. earlier this year opened its new Toyota Technical Center USA in Ann Arbor Township, where it now employs more than 500 people, about 80 percent of them Americans—a ratio that has flipped from 80 percent Japanese about a decade ago. And the company has added a new styling center in Ann Arbor as well.

Cost Savings That Benefit America

... The cost savings enjoyed by US companies are the most obvious source of value. For every dollar of corporate spending that moves offshore, US companies save 58 cents, and the quality of the services they buy is often higher: wages are lower, so companies can hire better-qualified people and spend more on supervision and training. Offshore workers are often more highly motivated than US workers and perform better, particularly in low-skilled jobs that lack prestige and suffer from high turnover in the United States. One British bank's call-center agents in India not only process 20 percent more transactions than their counterparts in the United Kingdom but also do so 3 percent more accurately.

Ultimately, in a competitive economy such as that of the United States, consumers benefit as companies pass on savings in the form of lower prices. New research by Catherine Mann, of the Institute for International Economics, in Washington, DC, found that the global sourcing of components has reduced the cost of IT [information technology] hardware by up to 30 percent since 1995, boosting demand and adding as much as $230 billion to the US GDP [gross domestic product] in that period. Trade in services will have similar effects. A technician in India, for instance, can read a magnetic-resonance-imaging (MRI) scan for a fraction of what it would cost in the United States. Transferring that position to India might cause a US medical technician to be laid off, but lower prices for life-saving technologies mean that more sick people can receive them.

The McKinsey Quarterly,
"Exploding the Myths of Offshoring," July 14, 2004.

Winning Hearts and Minds

Outsourcing, like trade in general, is reshaping the world in favorable ways beyond our borders. In a classic win-win from trade, outsourcing invigorates the U.S. economy at the same time it builds a pro-American middle class in India and other developing countries. The Indian high-tech sector is flourishing because that nation has adopted the U.S. model of zero tariffs on imported software and hardware, no restrictions on foreign investment, and an emphasis on post-secondary education.

While most of the jobs outsourced from the United States are on the lower end of the pay and status scales in the United States, they are among the best jobs available in India and other developing countries. In such cities as Bangalore, Calcutta, and New Delhi, hundreds of thousands of young Indian college graduates, men and women alike, are realizing the fruits of middle-class life that we take for granted. Although the $6,000 paid to an Indian programmer sounds ridiculously low in American terms, it can buy about five times as much in India because of lower domestic prices, enabling Indian programmers to rent their own apartments, own cell phones, make car payments, and travel abroad.

As the United States seeks to win friends and influence events in South Asia and elsewhere, it would be hard to find a more naturally pro-American enclave than the Indian high-tech sector. It would be terribly short sighted to disrupt our growing, mutually beneficial trade and security relationship with the world's most populous democracy to save a relatively small number of jobs that are not among the more well-paying in the Untied States.

Preserving the U.S. Free Trade Ideal

So far the rhetoric against outsourcing has been worse than any legislative action. The main vehicle against outsourcing has been restrictions on government contracts.... [In 2004],

Congress enacted a temporary ban on certain contracts with companies that would outsource the work abroad, and 30 states including Michigan are considering similar language for state contracts. Those restrictions on government procurement would come at a high price for the few jobs that would be saved.

First and most obvious, imposing anti-outsourcing restrictions on state contracting will waste state resources. Limiting the bidding for state contracts will only limit the state's ability to find the best deal for taxpayers, resulting in higher costs for state services. Restrictions on state contracts will force taxpayers either to pay more for the same services or to receive fewer services for the same cost. . . .

Second, restrictions on outsourcing will invite retaliation against the juicy target of U.S. service exporters and make a mockery of the U.S. government's calls for more opportunities for U.S. companies to bid competitively for government contracts abroad. Restrictions on outsourcing make the United States look even more hypocritical to the rest of the world. How can we urge other countries to lower their trade barriers and open bidding for government contracts to U.S. companies when we are trying to close our markets and government procurement to foreign suppliers?

Third, state restrictions on outsourcing may violate the U.S. Constitution and international law. Such laws could be challenged in court for usurping the power of the federal government to determine U.S. foreign policy and regulate international commerce. Similar state purchasing laws that had banned contracts with companies that do business in Burma (Myanmar) were nullified after being successfully challenged in the U.S. Supreme Court. As one recent legal study concluded, "Proposed state and federal legislation to restrict outsourcing may violate the U.S. Constitution and jeopardize U.S. obligations under international trade agreements."

Fourth, restrictions on outsourcing will reduce demand for U.S. products abroad. It will hinder development in countries such as India, slowing the expansion of a middle class able to afford U.S. goods and services. It will also deprive people outside of the United States of the additional dollars they could use as foreign exchange to buy U.S.-made goods and services or to invest in the U.S. economy. A barrier to imports is really a barrier to exports.

A Long-Term View of Economics and Outsourcing

It's difficult to gauge the true intensity of Americans' alarm over the job-offshoring phenomenon, both because the economy is only still recovering from a recession that especially pinched IT workers and because the issue emerged strongly into public discussion only during 2003, and thoroughly bathed in presidential politics.

Like changes in technology or consumer tastes, offshoring can disrupt the lives of certain workers, companies, and even entire communities. Michigan shares with the rest of the states in both the temporary and localized pain but also in the far greater and more lasting opportunities. And in all likelihood, the adjustments and the opportunities in [Michigan] and across the country created by offshoring will only grow in the years ahead.

Yet as participants and decision makers in the greatest economy the world has ever known, the changes brought by offshoring are just the most recent manifestation of a process that has always been an integral part of our dynamic, market-driven economy. Along the way, nearly all Americans—blessed with the best educational system and the most opportunity-laden marketplace ever known to man—will make the necessary changes in their own vocations and lives.

If the United States, its companies and its workers are to remain leaders in the global economy, offshoring must remain a tool available to our corporations—just as harnessing electricity was in the late 1800s, just as perfecting mass production was in the first half of the twentieth century, and just as the development of today's digital economy has been over the past few decades. Any shorter view of offshoring ultimately will prove self-defeating.

| *"The U.S. economy simply does not op-
erate as a large corporation."*

The Economic Benefits of Outsourcing Have Been Exaggerated

L. Josh Bivens

*In the following viewpoint, economist and Economic Policy Insti-
tute researcher L. Josh Bivens attempts to expose what he deems
questionable and exaggerated claims made in studies heralding
the benefits of outsourcing. He dissects the arguments set forth in
one prominent study, explaining why economic benefits for an
individual corporation do not necessarily translate into the same
degree of economic benefit on a national level. His largest concern is that this exaggeration of facts not only serves to confuse
the public about outsourcing's impact on the economy, but also
distracts from the more pressing problem—namely, that when it
comes to outsourcing, American workers are losers even if corporations benefit.*

L. Josh Bivens, "Truth and Consequences of Offshoring: Recent Studies Overstate the
Benefits and Ignore the Costs to American Workers," *EPI Briefing Paper #155*, August
2, 2005. Reproduced by permission.

As you read, consider the following questions:

1. Why should the 14 percent implicit rate of return esti-mated to result from outsourcing be considered care-fully, according to the author?
2. The author explains that the "terms of trade" will cause what type of impact on the United States economy as a result of outsourcing?
3. Studies championing outsourcing claim workers will be able to recoup the wages lost to outsourcing later as consumers in what ways?

Over the past two years, economic observers have focused attention on a new trend in the American economy: in-creased global competition for white-collar jobs that used to seem well-insulated and secure. While blue-collar labor (particularly in manufacturing) has felt a squeeze from global competition for decades, both in terms of employment secu-rity and wage growth, white-collar jobs held by well-credentialed Americans have been largely safe from pressures stemming from the global labor market. Recent reports of companies sending work abroad, ranging from call-center op-erators to software programmers, have changed this feeling of security.

Such insecurity, especially coming from a group that many assumed would be a prime beneficiary of globalization—i.e., well-credentialed, white-collar workers—has generated a po-tent political anxiety about the implications of global eco-nomic integration for American workers.

In response to this anxiety and an incipient political back-lash against offshoring, a number of studies have been re-leased by various organizations touting large economic ben-efits that will accrue to the American economy through the offshoring of white-collar work. A closer examination of these studies, however, shows that the promised benefits of offshor-ing are far overstated, while the likely economic costs are not addressed at all. Further, even the potential benefits to the American economy from offshoring are likely to be concentrated in the incomes of a relatively select percentage of American households. . . .

Calculating the Benefits of Outsourcing

The McKinsey Global Institute (MGI) is an independent economics think tank within the McKinsey & Company consulting firm. In 2003 it produced a report titled "Offshoring: Is It a Win-Win Game?" that received much media attention. More recently, this report's findings are reiterated and explained further in a short report titled "Exploding the Myths of Offshoring." The MGI reports identify large economic benefits that individual firms have already reaped from offshoring service production abroad. However, the report fails to make the case that these firm-level benefits will translate into net economy-wide gains. The U.S. economy simply does not operate as a large corporation, and pointing to cost savings realized by individual firms does not imply similar gains to national income.

The most well-known aspect of the MGI reports is a chart used to illustrate the potential benefits to the U.S. economy from offshoring. What MGI and proponents of offshoring have stressed is the last bar in the figure, which shows $1.14 in total benefits accruing to the United States from each dollar offshored. The precise breakdown of these benefits is described as follows:

- Fifty-eight cents is saved in corporate costs;

- U.S. exports to the country where employment has been offshored increases by five cents; and

- Four cents is repatriated to U.S. multinationals from the offshored location.

The above calculation totals 67 cents in benefits from each dollar offshored. Then, MGI estimates that workers laid-off in the U.S. will earn 47 cents for every dollar offshored when re-employed into the U.S. workforce generating $1.14 in total benefits to the U.S. economy from offshoring. One imagines that this figure is meant to be illustrative rather than presenting a last word on the empirical effect of outsourcing. That said, there are a number of things that are useful to note about it.

Individual Gains Versus National Gains

First, the implicit rate of return from engaging in offshoring (14%) identified in this example is enormous, and likely implausible for the U.S. economy at large. It is based, according to MGI, on a proprietary data set of firms that have already engaged in offshoring to India. As such, it is essentially a self-selected group of firms that have chosen to offshore their labor specifically because offshoring provides the largest economic gains. This rate of return, then, applies only to those firms for which offshoring would have the largest payoff; it is not the *average* payoff that could be expected from a representative U.S. firm sending work offshore.

Second, MGI fails to account for how the increased imports resulting from white-collar offshoring will be financed by the U.S. economy. An individual company need not concern itself with finding exports to offset its imports, but any analysis of the effects of offshoring on the U.S. economy must do so. In MGI's example . . . they assume that one dollar of goods previously produced domestically will now be offshored from abroad—meaning that imports into the United States will increase by one dollar. MGI assumes that this generates five cents worth of exports. But the other 95 cents of imports still has to be financed by increasing exports, which transfers resources (that could instead be used to support U.S. consumption and/or investment) to the rest of the world. MGI, by focusing only on a select group of firms instead of the wider economy, enumerates the benefits of offshoring (i.e., cost-savings gained from importing goods that once were produced domestically) while remaining silent on the costs (transferring domestic resources to finance increased imports).

Terms of Trade Dictate Economic Benefit

Third, while the firms that have already engaged in offshoring may have reaped large returns, this still does not mean that recent trends toward increased offshoring are an unambiguous windfall for the American economy. While it may make sense for an individual firm to offshore, if this practice becomes widespread enough to result in a rapid increase in foreign productivity in sectors in which the United States is a net exporter, this could actually result in a loss to U.S. income through *terms of trade effects*. This possibility describes precisely the situation that occurs when U.S. companies offshore production in high-skill professions that produce U.S. exports, such as software.

The *terms of trade* of the United States refer to the prices foreign purchasers pay for U.S. exports relative to the prices U.S. residents pay for imports. If U.S. exports fetch ever-higher prices on world markets and/or U.S. import prices drop, the terms of trade for the United States improve—the United States is able to consume more goods given its current income and productivity. If instead U.S. exports fetch ever-lower prices and/or imports become more expensive, U.S. terms of trade deteriorate and its residents are able to consume less given current income and productivity.

To take a concrete example, assume that the United States only exports software programs (as its trading partners are unable to produce these) and that it only imports oil (as the U.S. has none of its own). As oil becomes more expensive, U.S. residents are made unambiguously worse off; they pay more as consumers but do not gain anything as producers. Now, imagine that U.S. trading partners are able to start producing software programs, and the increased supply of these

Offshoring of Services vs. Offshoring of Manufacturing

When the offshoring of services truly hits (and it will stretch out over several decades), it is likely to deliver a much greater shock to the U.S. economy than the offshoring of manufacturing did. There are several reasons for this. First, in the 1970s, Americans' incomes exceeded those of the Japanese by a ratio of about two to one. The ratio of American to Indian incomes today is more than ten to one.... [Therefore,] the potential pay cuts for workers who lose out in rich countries will also be that much greater.

Second, the coming global trade in services will potentially affect a much larger proportion of the U.S. labor force. Even at its height, manufacturing constituted only 28 percent of all non-farm employment, and large sectors of manufacturing (food processing, for example) are closely tied to sources of supply and thus immovable. Service jobs constitute 83 percent of non-farm employment in the U.S. economy today, and every job that is (or could be) defined largely by the use of computers and telephones will be vulnerable.

Third, the impact of foreign competition will be borne much more directly by American workers than by their employers. In the 1970s and 1980s, foreign imports threatened U.S. companies and workers equally. The CEOs at GM and Ford were on the same "side" as the men and women who worked on the factory floor. The coming wave of economic dislocation will look very different: it will be something that American CEOs do to their own workers.

Stephen S. Cohen and J. Bradford Delong, "Shaken and Stirred,"
Atlantic Monthly, *January-February 2005.*

services drives down their price. The United States could then actually be worse off if the loss to domestic producers of software from lower prices swamps the beneficial impact of lower prices to U.S. consumers.

While offshoring of white-collar work may provide benefits to individual firms, if it becomes widespread enough to lead to rapid productivity gains in sectors in which the United States is a prime exporter, the U.S. terms of trade could deteriorate enough to cause actual income losses for the country. Even if this does not occur, the terms of trade effect could still lean against any efficiency gain from offshoring, leading to a smaller economy-wide effect than suggested by the firm-level analysis of MGI.

Workers and Consumers Still Lose

Fourth, and perhaps most importantly, even MGI's own numbers point to something striking about the pattern of benefits to be reaped from offshoring: *American workers are net losers.* This can be seen by comparing the "savings accrued to U.S. investors and/or customers" to the "value from U.S. labor re-employed." The cost savings from offshoring to low-wage locales is 58 cents, while U.S. workers end up with only 47 cents in labor earnings after the fact. This implies a loss of 11 cents for labor earnings from each dollar of production that is offshored, money that is a pure redistribution of income away from U.S. workers. MGI correctly identifies the benefits of this redistribution as accruing to capital incomes (greater profits) or lower prices. If the redistribution goes strictly to capital-owners, then workers are unambiguously worse off (assuming that workers earn little income from capital-holdings). If the latter scenario occurs, and some of this redistribution forces down prices, then workers can recoup some of their lost wages as consumers purchasing at these lower prices.

The degree to which this money goes to price declines (which benefit consumers) versus enhanced corporate profits (which hurt the average worker) is largely unknown. However, it is clearly the case that the current recovery is the most unbalanced on record in regards to wages growth versus growth in corporate profits. . . .

Further, even if some of the corporate savings manifested as price declines, this would still not necessarily lead to higher living standards for American households. A commonly identified reason for the continued lagging of growth in labor compensation behind growth in productivity in recent decades is the persistent gap between inflation in the prices of goods *consumed* by American households relative to the price of goods *produced* by American workers. . . .

Whether offshoring-induced price declines show up as improved living standards for American households is an open question, dependent upon how intensively these households consume the services that are being offshored.

Carefully Considering the Data

The MGI study makes the assumption that what is good for the subset of U.S. corporations that have already engaged in offshoring of services abroad can be scaled up to predict gains for the U.S. economy as a whole. This ignores offsetting costs to the U.S. economy of terms of trade effects and the need to finance growing imports. Further, even if the U.S. economy reaps efficiency gains from offshoring, these are unlikely to accrue to American workers. . . .

The issue of offshoring demands a careful response by policy makers, with the great challenge being to make sure any potential benefits are equitably distributed among firms and workers. Any policy response must therefore be well informed about the costs and benefits of offshoring. Proponents of offshoring and many economists have claimed that its negative impact on the U.S. economy over the past four years has been exaggerated by politicians and others. Even if true, this ignores the fact that offshoring is likely to grow rapidly in the future and could well have large effects on the U.S. economy in years to come. Therefore, balanced analyses about what these effects would be are needed. The three reports examined in this paper exaggerate the size of the benefits offered to American workers by offshoring and gloss over the more troubling distributional consequences.

While offshoring has clearly provided substantial cost savings and improved profits for a number of firms that have engaged in it, one cannot assume that these benefits will scale up for the broader economy. Mainstream international economics teaches that deepening international integration *usually* increases national income, but not always. The offshoring of white-collar work and its consequences (i.e., foreign productivity growth in what is an export sector for the United States) fits in with many of the characteristics of the exceptions.

"The issue of outsourcing overseas is neither new nor is it as overwhelming as some suggest."

History Confirms That Outsourcing Fears Are Exaggerated

Milton Ezrati

Economist Milton Ezrati argues in the following viewpoint that the outsourcing of jobs overseas is not a recent phenomenon. In fact, Ezrati states that American workers have been facing competition from workers overseas since the 1950s and 1960s. He chronicles the prior eras and fears, and contends that in each case innovation and productivity helped the American economy to grow and eventually create new and better jobs for American workers. Ezrati maintains that historically the U.S. economy has endured both prosperity and economic downturn without intervention, and he cautions against protectionist economic policies that would impose increased restrictions on trade between the United States and other nations.

Milton Ezrati, "Misplaced Fears: Why the Outsourcing Scare Is Overblown," *The International Economy*, vol. 18, Fall 2004, pp. 79–81. Copyright © 2004 International Economy Publications, Inc. Reproduced by permission.

As you read, consider the following questions:

1. What historic examples of "frightening projections" relating to jobs and the economy are mentioned by the author?

2. What jobs have been threatened by "labor-saving techniques" as opposed to outsourcing, according to the author?

3. According to the Commerce Department's Bureau of Economic Analysis, how much have workers' standards of living improved over past years?

Although the media for the time being has shed its panic over the outsourcing of jobs abroad, the issue nonetheless remains dangerous, not to American jobs directly, that was always overblown, but because the fear of outsourcing presents a powerful and ongoing political temptation to protectionism [an economic policy characterized by restrictive trading policies between nations]. . . . Even a hint that the United States might withdraw support for the world's free-trade regime (painstakingly developed during past decades) threatens global growth prospects and consequently more American jobs than any Chinese toy factory or Indian call center could. It is critically important, then, to put this situation into perspective.

The issue of outsourcing overseas is neither new nor is it as overwhelming as some suggest. At base, it is just the latest installment in the long-standing challenge to the United States from cheap foreign labor, one that began in the 1950s, when European wages were low, and has continued over time with a shifting focus to various countries. Since it is not new, it does not require new solutions, especially a dangerous protectionist response. The United States has managed throughout this long time without resorting to protectionism. It has instead met the challenge of cheap foreign labor successfully with impressive gains in labor productivity and ongoing innovation. The country can do the same in the present instance, too.

Competition Does Exist

There can be little doubt that today's challenge from low foreign wages is as great as it has ever been. A few simple comparisons illustrate. According to IBM [International Business Machines Corporation] a Chinese programmer with three to five years of experience earns the equivalent of around $12.50 an hour. His American equivalent makes closer to $56.00 an hour. American firms operating in Bangalore, India, note that a software engineer there makes about $30,000 per year, less than one-sixth of his Silicon Valley [region in Northern California known for its high concentration of high-tech business] equivalent. The average English-speaking telephone operator in India makes about $1.50 an hour, compared with $11.00 for a similar operator in the States.

Such vast wage differences seem insurmountable and lead naturally to frightening views of a future full of unemployment and poverty. Feeding that fear is a report from the Gartner Group, an independent consulting firm. It indicates that some 80 percent of American boards of directors have responded to such wage differentials by discussing outsourcing offshore. More than 40 percent have completed some sort of a pilot project. Forrester Research, another private consulting group, estimates that this country will export a total of 3.3 million white-collar jobs by 2015, including 1.7 million back-office jobs and 473,000 positions in information technology. The Department of Commerce has extrapolated recent trends in outsourcing and estimated that service imports of legal work, computer programming, telecommunications, banking, engineering, and management consulting will rise rapidly from . . . [2003's] level of about $17.4 billion to erase the country's trade surplus in services in just a few years.

A History of Alarmist Predictions

But such frightening projections are nothing new. For more than half a century, wage differentials between the United

States and some foreign rival have always seemed insurmountable, at least at first, and people have feared the worst. In the 1950s and 1960s, financial journalists and politicians fretted that the country would lose all its manufacturing to low-wage German labor. It is hard today to think of German labor as cheap, but it was back then. After the European scare, there was Japan, with automobiles in the 1970s and more generally in the 1980s. It, too, occasioned dire predictions. Then it was Mexico and now China and India. At each phase, of course, ongoing changes in technology and the economies of the world rendered different jobs vulnerable. The particular institutional arrangements altered, too. With Europe and Japan, the competition came mostly from foreign firms, whereas more recently, it has come from American firms subcontracting to their own foreign subsidiaries. But at base, the story has consistently been one of low-cost foreign labor.

At each phase during this long period, the forecasts of disaster sound remarkably like today's doomsaying. John Kennedy, for example, in his 1960 presidential campaign, spoke of foreign competition carrying "the dark menace of industrial dislocation, increasing unemployment, and deepening poverty." Twenty years later, when the threat came from Japan, prominent financier Felix Rohatyn talked about, "de-industrialization" and the prospect of America becoming, "a nation of short-order cooks and saleswomen." At that same time, then-Senator Lloyd Bentsen worried: "American workers will end up like the people in the biblical village who were condemned to be hewers of wood and drawers of water." A short while later, Walter Mondale, while serving as U.S. ambassador to Japan, suggested that Americans would soon be fit only to sweep the floors in Japanese factories. By the late 1980s, when Japan was beginning to fall into stagnation and the foreign threat had shifted to Mexico, then presidential candidate Ross Perot could hear the "giant sucking sound" of lost jobs. On the verge of the great technological leap of the

1990s, a Pulitzer Prize went to two journalists, Donald L. Barlett and James B. Steele, for their book on America's decline, *America: What Went Wrong.*

Almost all these ugly outlooks have come equipped with calls for protectionist measures. Fortunately, the nation has resisted this misguided political solution. The United States instead has coped by applying its genius for productivity enhancement. Ever-higher levels of productivity allowed American workers to warrant their relatively high wages, even if it meant fewer workers on a given project. And the country has coped through technological innovation and product development to create new jobs for otherwise displaced workers in new and previously unimagined industries and pursuits.

Innovation and Productivity Drive Growth

The stress on productivity probably would have occurred even without foreign competition. American producers would still have responded to this country's high wages with robotics and other labor-saving techniques. Their efforts would still have raised the productivity of some workers and forced layoffs on others. Receptionists, after all, have faced a similar experience from the introduction of voice mail, even though foreign competition has hardly applied to them. The same could be said for bank tellers and ATM machines. Middle management has faced the same from improved systems and communications, even in those areas where foreign competition is not an issue. Some of the jobs lost to automation and systems have, of course, reappeared overseas, not because they were stolen, but rather because the low wages abroad relieve those operations of any need for labor saving techniques. Either way, high-paid American labor has lost the jobs.

Those displaced by heightened productivity, whether inspired by foreign competition or not, have suffered until ultimately innovation created new industries with new employment opportunities. Throughout the transition, of course,

Outsourcing Is Different from Direct Foreign Investment

In the public controversy over outsourcing and its effects on American prosperity, jobs and wages, at least two phenomena have been muddled up with the purchase of long-distance services . . . , making the discussion of the outsourcing phenomenon opaque and misleading, to say the least.

First, the public outcry often slides over into imports of all services. . . . Sometimes the critics of outsourcing appear to include even the imports by firms of manufacturing components, as under the early-1980s definition of "outsourcing." In fact, such enlargement of the scope of the phenomenon of outsourcing should include imports of products for final consumption as well: after all, there is no difference in principle between an American factory owner importing French brie and Burgundy for his supper, instead of consuming Milwaukee beer and Kraft cheese, and his importing a Japanese lathe rather than one manufactured in Ohio for his factory in Youngstown. Second, the phenomenon of direct foreign investment [in which companies build factories or other facilities in countries outside their home country or purchase shares of a foreign company] is often added indiscriminately to the discussion of outsourcing . . . , as when a firm closes its plant in Boston and invests in production in Bombay, or when a firm simply opens up a factory in Nairobi instead of in Nantucket. . . .

Jagdish Bhagwati, Arvind Panagariya, and T.N. Srinivasan,
"The Muddles over Outsourcing,"
Journal of Economic Perspectives, *Fall 2004.*

people have doubted that the new industries and new jobs would develop. That is understandable, since at any point in time it is difficult to envision where innovation will take the economy. In the 1950s and 1960s, for instance, when cheap European labor threatened America's traditional steel industry, few could imagine how the telecommunications and technological revolutions of the last forty years would employ millions in previously undreamed of jobs. In the 1970s and 1980s, when Japanese competition threatened employment in the auto industry and some of the new areas of technology, people could not see how innovation in this country would create a separate revolution in finance that transformed an industry dominated by bank clerks into one that employs millions at all levels, many in high-paying advisory positions that did not exist even twenty years ago. Similarly, cable and direct television have made their own employment revolution, creating jobs for millions at all skill and pay levels from technicians to executives. These are only the most obvious illustrations of the opportunities that have absorbed many of those displaced from more traditional industries for whatever reason.

With this innovation and productivity growth, the United States has put the lie to those ongoing forecasts of unemployment and poverty. Instead, the country has become more prosperous. In the past twenty years, for example, the growth of the information economy has created an 80 percent increase in management positions from 23.6 million in the early 1980s to 42.5 million [in 2004]. The proportion of such challenging, high-paying jobs has risen from 23.4 percent of the workforce to 31.1 percent. Testifying even more broadly to the effectiveness of productivity growth and innovation, the nation's standard of living has risen throughout this time, and impressively so. According to the Commerce Department's Bureau of Economic Analysis, per capita income [in 2003] averaged $28,215, up 175 percent in real terms from 1960, 58 percent from 1980, and almost 20 percent even from the boom year 1996. Clearly, most workers, if not every one, are doing better than they once were, despite the foreign competition.

The Lessons of History

For all the opportunity, there is no denying that the transitions forced by these patterns have also imposed great hardship on groups of workers and regions of the country. These deserve attention. But it is misguided to extrapolate such hardship to make endless warnings of general economic collapse and call for protectionist measures, especially in the face of the remarkably successful historic record. Looking forward, there is, of course, always the risk that the solutions of the past will fail, that the productivity growth will falter or the innovation fade. But the prospects of such a radical departure from past trends is not especially likely. Even though few today have the clairvoyance to paint a definite picture of future innovations and the new job opportunities, the long record of the past certainly raises the odds that they will occur and that the country will cope without the need to resort to protectionism.

> *"If we economists stubbornly insist on chanting 'Free trade is good for you' . . . we will quickly become irrelevant to the public debate."*

The Problems of Outsourcing Are Unprecedented

Alan S. Blinder

In the following viewpoint, Alan S. Blinder defends his stance that the outsourcing of American jobs is unprecedented at its current pace and explains his apprehension toward embracing this aspect of free trade. He voices concern with the way in which economists continually offer theoretical explanations for the benefits of free trade to people who are losing their jobs as a result of the open market system. Further, the author worries that the period of coming transition resulting from the outsourcing of service jobs, previously immune to outsourcing, will prove especially difficult if the government does not work to provide support for those workers who lose their jobs. Alan S. Blinder is an economics professor at Princeton University.

Alan S. Blinder, "Free Trade's Great, but Offshoring Rattles Me," *The Washington Post*, May 6, 2007, p. B04. Copyright © 2007 The Washington Post Company. Reproduced by permission of the author.

As you read, consider the following questions:

1. According to Blinder, what two "powerful, historical forces" are responsible for the changes in international trade?
2. What does the author claim will be new about the coming transition to service offshoring?
3. The author believes that the education system should prepare people for what jobs?

I'm a free trader down to my toes. Always have been. Yet lately, I'm being treated as a heretic by many of my fellow economists. Why? Because I have stuck my neck out and predicted that the offshoring of service jobs from rich countries such as the United States to poor countries such as India may pose major problems for tens of millions of American workers over the coming decades. In fact, I think offshoring may be the biggest political issue in economics for a generation.

When I say this, many of my fellow free-traders react with a mixture of disbelief, pity and hostility. Blinder, have you lost your mind? (Answer: I think not.) Have you forgotten about the basic economic gains from international trade? (Answer: *No*.) Are you advocating some form of protectionism? (Answer: *No!*) Aren't you giving aid and comfort to the enemies of free trade? (Answer: No, I'm trying to save free trade from itself.)

The reason for my alleged apostasy [rejection of beliefs] is that the nature of international trade is changing before our eyes. We used to think, roughly, that an item was tradable only if it could be put in a box and shipped. That's no longer true. Nowadays, a growing list of services can be zapped across international borders electronically. It's electrons that move, not boxes. We're all familiar with call centers, but electronic service delivery has already extended to computer programming, a variety of engineering services, accounting, security analysis and a lot else. And much more is on the way.

Why do I say much more? Because two powerful, historical forces are driving these changes, and both are virtually certain to grow stronger over time.

The Two Factors Driving Change

The first is technology, especially information and communications technology, which has been improving at an astonishing pace in recent decades. As the technology advances, the quality of now-familiar modes of communication (such as telephones, videoconferencing and the Internet) will improve, and entirely new forms of communication may be invented. One clear implication of the upward march of technology is that a widening army of services will become deliverable electronically from afar. And it's not just low-skill services such as key punching, transcription and telemarketing. It's also high-skill services such as radiology, architecture and engineering—maybe even college teaching.

The second driver is the entry of about 1.5 billion "new" workers into the world economy. These folks aren't new to the world, of course. But they live in places such as China, India and the former Soviet bloc—countries that used to stand outside the world economy. For those who say, "Sure, but most of them are low-skilled workers," I have two answers. First, even a small percentage of 1.5 billion people is a lot of folks. And second, India and China will certainly educate hundreds of millions more in the coming decades. So there will be a lot of willing and able people available to do the jobs that technology will move offshore.

Looking at these two historic forces from the perspective of the world as a whole, one can only get a warm feeling. Improvements in technology will raise living standards, just as they have since the dawn of the Industrial Revolution. And the availability of millions of new electronically deliverable service jobs in, say, India and China will help alleviate poverty on a mass scale. Offshoring will also reduce costs and boost productivity in the United States. So repeat after me: Globalization is good for the world. Which is where economists usually stop.

And where my alleged apostasy starts.

For these same forces don't look so benign from the viewpoint of an American computer programmer or accountant. They've done what they were told to do: They went to college and prepared for well-paid careers with bountiful employment opportunities. But now their bosses are eyeing legions of well-qualified, English-speaking programmers and accountants in India, for example, who will happily work for a fraction of what Americans earn. Such prospective competition puts a damper on wage increases. And if the jobs do move offshore, displaced American workers may lose not only their jobs but also their pensions and health insurance. These people can be forgiven if they have doubts about the virtues of globalization.

An Unprecedented Transitional Period

We economists assure folks that things will be all right in the end. Both Americans and Indians will be better off. I think that's right. The basic principles of free trade that Adam Smith and David Ricardo taught us two centuries ago remain valid today: Just like people, nations benefit by specializing in the tasks they do best and trading with other nations for the rest. There's nothing new here theoretically.

But I would argue that there's something new about the coming transition to service offshoring. Those two powerful forces mentioned earlier—technological advancement and the rise of China and India—suggest that this particular transition will be large, lengthy and painful.

It's going to be lengthy because the technology for moving information across the world will continue to improve for decades, if not forever. So, for those who earn their living performing tasks that are (or will become) deliverable electronically, this is no fleeting problem.

Building Companies with Outsourcing

In theory, it is becoming possible to buy, off the shelf, practically any function you need to run a company. Want to start a budget airline but don't want to invest in a huge back office? [Consulting and outsourcing company] Accenture's Navitaire unit can manage reservations, plan routes, assign crew, and calculate optimal prices for each seat.

... For about $5,000, analytics outfits such as New Delhi-based Evalueserve Inc. will, within a day, assemble a team of Indian patent attorneys, engineers, and business analysts, start mining global databases, and call dozens of U.S. experts and wholesalers to provide an independent appraisal.

Want to market quickly a new mutual fund or insurance policy? IT [information technology] services providers such as India's Tata Consultancy Services Ltd. are building software platforms that furnish every business process needed and secure all regulatory approvals. A sister company, Tata Technologies, can now handle everything from turning a conceptual design into detailed specs for interiors, chassis, and electrical systems to designing the tooling and factory-floor layout. . . .

Few big companies have tried all these options yet. But some, like Procter & Gamble [a consumer products company manufacturing items ranging from soap to prescription drugs to disposable diapers], are showing that the ideas are not far-fetched. Over the past three years the $57 billion consumer-products company has outsourced everything from IT infrastructure and human resources to management of its offices from Cincinnati to Moscow. . . .

Pete Engardio, "The Future of Outsourcing,"
Business Week, January 30, 2006.

It's also going to be large. How large? In some recent research, I estimated that 30 million to 40 million U.S. jobs are potentially offshorable. These include scientists, mathematicians and editors on the high end and telephone operators, clerks and typists on the low end. Obviously, not all of these jobs are going to India, China or elsewhere. But many will.

It's going to be painful because our country offers such a poor social safety net to cushion the blow for displaced workers. Our unemployment insurance program is stingy by first-world standards. American workers who lose their jobs often lose their health insurance and pension rights as well. And even though many displaced workers will have to change occupations—a difficult task for anyone—only a fortunate few will be offered opportunities for retraining. All this needs to change.

Keeping Economists' Views Relevant

What else is to be done? Trade protection won't work. You can't block electrons from crossing national borders. Because U.S. labor cannot compete on price, we must reemphasize the things that have kept us on top of the economic food chain for so long: technology, innovation, entrepreneurship, adaptability and the like. That means more science and engineering, more spending on R&D [research and development], keeping our capital markets big and vibrant, and not letting ourselves get locked into "sunset" industries [industries that produce products or services no longer in high demand].

In addition, we need to rethink our education system so that it turns out more people who are trained for the jobs that will remain in the United States and fewer for the jobs that will migrate overseas. We cannot, of course, foresee exactly which jobs will go and which will stay. But one good bet is that many electronic service jobs will move offshore, whereas personal service jobs will not. Here are a few examples. Tax accounting is easily offshorable; onsite auditing is not. Computer programming is offshorable; computer repair is not. Ar-chitects could be endangered, but builders aren't. Were it not for stiff regulations, radiology would be offshorable; but pedi-atrics and geriatrics aren't. Lawyers who write contracts can do so at a distance and deliver them electronically; litigators who argue cases in court cannot.

But even if we do everything I've suggested—which we won't—American workers will still face a troublesome transi-tion as tens of millions of old jobs are replaced by new ones. There will also be great political strains on the open trading system as millions of white-collar workers who thought their jobs were immune to foreign competition suddenly find that the game has changed—and not to their liking.

That is why I am going public with my concerns now. If we economists stubbornly insist on chanting "Free trade is good for you" to people who know that it is not, we will quickly become irrelevant to the public debate. Compared with that, a little apostasy should be welcome.

Periodical Bibliography

The following articles have been selected to supplement the diverse views presented in this chapter.

William J. Amelio   "Beyond Outsourcing, to Worldsourcing," *Business Week*, May 30, 2008. www.businessweek-.com.

Clive Crook   "Beyond Belief," *Atlantic Monthly*, October 2007.

Pete Engardio et al.   "Can the U.S. Bring Jobs Back from China?" *Business Week*, June 30, 2008.

Steve Hamm   "Outsourcing's Dubious Kingmakers," *Business Week*, July 14, 2008.

Brad Kenney   "Offshoring in Reverse," *Industry Week/IW*, October 2007.

M.S. Krishnan   "More than Cost Benefits," *Information Week*, May 12, 2008.

George Leopold   "Offshoring: Risk to U.S. Innovation?" *Electronic Engineering Times*, November 27, 2006.

Michael Mandel, Steve Hamm, and Christopher Farrell   "Are They Good for America?" *Business Week*, March 10, 2008.

Mary K. Pratt   "Ethical Outsourcing," *Computerworld*, April 21, 2008.

Rob Preston   "Global Outsourcing Not a One-Way Street from U.S.," *Information Week*, August 13, 2007.

Jonathan Whitaker, M.S. Krishnan, and Claes Fornell   "How Offshore Outsourcing Affects Customer Satisfaction," *Wall Street Journal*, July 7, 2008.

Ben Worthen   "Competitive Approach Taken to Outsourcing," *Wall Street Journal*, May 20, 2008.

OPPOSING
VIEWPOINTS®
SERIES

CHAPTER 2

What Is the Impact of Outsourcing on National Security?

Chapter Preface

In mid-2008 an estimated 148,000 U.S. troops remain in Iraq to combat guerrilla resistance and keep order. In addition to the national military forces still engaged in this ongoing conflict, a contingent of private contractors has added its strength to allied operations. These contractors have provided everything from support tasks, such as cooking and cleaning for soldiers, to weapons upkeep and security. While the Iraq War does not mark the first time the U.S. government has outsourced military duties to the private sector, the scale of contracting in this conflict, and the controversy generated by the deployment of private companies, has led to an ongoing public debate over the role of private military firms in a conflict that supposedly has national security implications. As the war has continued much longer than originally estimated, these private forces are steeped in the struggle and play a critical role in the ongoing occupation of the country.

Critics of military outsourcing with regard to the Iraq War cite numerous examples of unsavory conduct by private corporation personnel to support their claims that the private sector should not be taking on roles traditionally performed by the military. Specifically, they point to the trespasses at the Abu Ghraib prison in Iraq, in which inmates thought to have terrorist connections were injured, humiliated, and tortured by U.S. soldiers and support crews. On June 30, 2008, lawsuits were filed against CACI International, Inc., and its subsidiaries, alleging that employees of the corporation played a role in the interrogations and mistreatment that occurred in the prison.

Aside from these allegations, critics also point to instances in which private contractors doing technical and maintenance jobs were implicated in deaths of Americans. For example, detractors refer to the lack of oversight that allowed contractor

Kellog, Brown, and Root (KBR) to file reports stating that military bases suffered from poor electrical wiring and yet the company did nothing to fix it because their contract called for repair of the electrical system only in the event of failure, not for regular maintenance. Faulty wiring was deemed the cause of the electrocution deaths of twelve military personnel since the war's outset.

Many proponents, however, maintain that government outsourcing to private contractors is necessary if the United States is to be successful in its military pursuits. Career Army officer and executive vice president of the Council on Foreign Relations Michael P. Peters has stated, "It's a virtual necessity, given the state and size of the military, to outsource." Others, such as Marvin Leibstone emphasize the financial savings provided by military outsourcing; he writes in the journal *Military Technology* that the cost of the Iraq War would be "billions of dollars higher" without outsourcing. Further, Leibstone states that outsourcing has helped to prevent the reinstatement of a civilian draft to meet the manpower needs of the military.

These critiques and praises of the private military industry represent only parts of the debate concerning outsourcing in the current Iraq War. While the costs and benefits, both financial and ethical, of military outsourcing in the war will continue to be weighed, these questions fall within a much larger discussion over the impact of outsourcing on American national security. The authors in the following chapter debate whether outsourcing will make the country safer in the long run and whether outsourcing is appropriate for military operations and national security matters.

> "[Private military firms] represent . . .
> the corporate evolution of the age-old
> profession of mercenaries."

Outsourcing Military Duties to Private Contractors Is Problematic

Peter W. Singer

In the following viewpoint, Peter W. Singer argues that private military firms (PMFs) are a problematic industry for governments worldwide. While he concedes that they have aided in certain combat and military support situations, Singer outlines the numerous problems that the outsourcing of public military duties to private firms has created in recent years. He maintains that unless governments find new ways to define and regulate this industry, contracting with PMFs will continue to be a risk to military operations globally. A senior fellow at the Brookings Institution, Peter W. Singer is also the author of the books Corporate Warriors: The Rise of the Privatized Military Industry *and* Children at War.

Peter W. Singer, "Outsourcing War," *Foreign Affairs*, vol. 84, March–April 2005, pp. 119–132. Copyright © 2008 by the Council on Foreign Relations, Inc. All rights reserved. Reprinted by permission of Foreign Affairs, www.foreignaffairs.org.

As you read, consider the following questions:

1. What does Singer identify as the factors that drove the growth of the private military industry following the end of the cold war?

2. How, according to the author, has the use of PMFs in Iraq changed the way in which the George W. Bush administration has proceeded with the war there?

3. Singer states that the outsourcing of military operations has changed the armed forces in what ways?

The tales of war, profit, honor, and greed that emerge from the private military industry often read like something out of a Hollywood screenplay. They range from action-packed stories of guns-for-hire fighting off swarms of insurgents in Iraq to the sad account of a private military air crew languishing in captivity in Colombia, abandoned by their corporate bosses in the United States. A recent African "rent-a-coup" scandal involved the son of a former British prime minister, and accusations of war profiteering have reached into the halls of the White House itself.

Incredible as these stories often sound, the private military industry is no fiction. Private companies are becoming significant players in conflicts around the world, supplying not merely the goods but also the services of war. Although recent well-publicized incidents from Abu Ghraib[1] to Zimbabwe[2] have shone unaccustomed light onto this new force in warfare, private military firms (PMFs) remain a poorly understood—and often unacknowledged—phenomenon. Mystery, myth, and conspiracy theory surround them, leaving policy makers and the public in positions of dangerous ignorance. Many key questions remain unanswered, including, What is

1. Interrogators from private firms contracted by the U.S. government who abused prisoners and engaged in other questionable behaviors.
2. Employees of the private military company Logo Logistics were arrested under allegations that they were transporting weapons to support a coup plot in Equatorial Guinea.

this industry and where did it come from? What is its role in the United States' largest current overseas venture, Iraq? What are the broader implications of that role? And how should policy makers respond? Only by developing a better understanding of this burgeoning industry can governments hope to get a proper hold on this newly powerful force in foreign policy. If they fail, the consequences for policy and democracy could be deeply destructive.

Post-Cold War, Private Military Firms Emerge

PMFs are businesses that provide governments with professional services intricately linked to warfare; they represent, in other words, the corporate evolution of the age-old profession of mercenaries. Unlike the individual dogs of war of the past, however, PMFs are corporate bodies that offer a wide range of services, from tactical combat operations and strategic planning to logistical support and technical assistance.

The modern private military industry emerged at the start of the 1990s, driven by three dynamics: the end of the Cold War, transformations in the nature of warfare that blurred the lines between soldiers and civilians, and a general trend toward privatization and outsourcing of government functions around the world. These three forces fed into each other. When the face-off between the United States and the Soviet Union ended, professional armies around the world were downsized. At the same time, increasing global instability created a demand for more troops. Warfare in the developing world also became messier—more chaotic and less professional—involving forces ranging from warlords to child soldiers, while Western powers became more reluctant to intervene. Meanwhile, advanced militaries grew increasingly reliant on off-the-shelf commercial technology, often maintained and operated by private firms. And finally, many governments succumbed to an ideological trend toward the privatization of many of their functions; a whole raft of former state responsibilities—including education, policing, and the operation of prisons—were turned over to the marketplace.

The PMFs that arose as a result are not all alike, nor do they all offer the exact same services. The industry is divided into three basic sectors: military provider firms (also known as "private security firms"), which offer tactical military assistance, including actual combat services, to clients; military consulting firms, which employ retired officers to provide strategic advice and military training; and military support firms, which provide logistics, intelligence, and maintenance services to armed forces, allowing the latter's soldiers to concentrate on combat and reducing their government's need to recruit more troops or call up more reserves.

Although the world's most dominant military has become increasingly reliant on PMFs (the Pentagon has entered into more than 3,000 such contracts over the last decade), the industry and its clientele are not just American. Private military companies have operated in more than 50 nations, on every continent but Antarctica. For example, European militaries, which lack the means to transport and support their forces overseas, are now greatly dependent on PMFs for such functions. To get to Afghanistan, European troops relied on a Ukrainian firm that, under a contract worth more than $100 million, ferried them there in former Soviet jets. And the British military, following in the Pentagon's footsteps, has begun to contract out its logistics to Halliburton.

The "Coalition of the Billing"

Nowhere has the role of PMFs been more integral—and more controversial—than in Iraq. Not only is Iraq now the site of the single largest U.S. military commitment in more than a decade; it is also the marketplace for the largest deployment of PMFs and personnel ever. More than 60 firms currently employ more than 20,000 private personnel there to carry out military functions (these figures do not include the thousands more that provide nonmilitary reconstruction and oil services)—roughly the same number as are provided by all of the United States' coalition partners combined. President George W. Bush's "coalition of the willing" might thus be more aptly described as the "coalition of the billing."

These large numbers have incurred large risks. Private military contractors have suffered an estimated 175 deaths and 900 wounded [as of March 2005] in Iraq (precise numbers are unavailable because the Pentagon does not track nonmilitary casualties)—more than any single U.S. Army division and more than the rest of the coalition combined.

More important than the raw numbers is the wide scope of critical jobs that contractors are now carrying out, far more extensive in Iraq than in past wars. In addition to war-gaming and field training U.S. troops before the invasion, private military personnel handled logistics and support during the war's buildup. The massive U.S. complex at Camp Doha in Kuwait, which served as the launch pad for the invasion, was not only built by a PMF but also operated and guarded by one. During the invasion, contractors maintained and loaded many of the most sophisticated U.S. weapons systems, such as B-2 stealth bombers and Apache helicopters. They even helped operate combat systems such as the Army's Patriot missile batteries and the Navy's Aegis missile-defense system.

PMFs—ranging from well-established companies such as Vinnell and mpri to startups such as the South African firm Erinys International—have played an even greater role in the postinvasion occupation and counterinsurgency effort. Halliburton's Kellogg, Brown & Root division, the largest corporate PMF in Iraq, currently provides supplies for troops and maintenance for equipment under a contract thought to be worth as much as $13 billion. (This figure, in current dollars, is roughly two and a half times what the United States paid to fight the entire 1991 Persian Gulf War, and roughly the same as what it spent to fight the American Revolution, the War of 1812, the Mexican-American War, and the Spanish-American War combined.) Other PMFs are helping to train local forces, including the new Iraqi army and national police, and are playing a range of tactical military roles.

An estimated 6,000 non-Iraqi private contractors currently carry out armed tactical functions in the country. These individuals are sometimes described as "security guards," but they are a far cry from the rent-a-cops who troll the food courts of U.S. shopping malls. In Iraq, their jobs include protecting important installations, such as corporate enclaves, U.S. facilities, and the Green Zone in Baghdad; guarding key individuals (Ambassador Paul Bremer, the head of the Coalition Provisional Authority, was protected by a Blackwater team that even had its own armed helicopters); and escorting convoys, a particularly dangerous task thanks to the frequency of roadside ambushes and bombings by the insurgents.

PMFs, in other words, have been essential to the U.S. effort in Iraq, helping Washington make up for its troop shortage and doing jobs that U.S. forces would prefer not to. But they have also been involved in some of the most controversial aspects of the war, including alleged corporate profiteering and abuse of Iraqi prisoners.

Private Military Firms and the Public Interest

The mixed record of PMFs in Iraq points to some of the underlying problems and questions related to the industry's increasing role in U.S. policy. Five broad policy dilemmas are raised by the increasing privatization of the military.

The first involves the question of profit in a military context. To put it bluntly, the incentives of a private company do not always align with its clients' interests—or the public good. In an ideal world, this problem could be kept in check through proper management and oversight; in reality, such scrutiny is often absent. As a result, war-profiteering allegations have been thrown at several firms. For example, Halliburton—Vice President Dick Cheney's previous employer—has been accused of a number of abuses in Iraq, ranging from overcharging for gasoline to billing for services not rendered; the disputed charges now total $1.8 billion. And Custer Battles, a startup military provider firm that was featured on the front page of the *Wall Street Journal* in August 2004 has since been accused of running a fraudulent scheme of subsidiaries and false charges.

Still more worrisome from a policy standpoint is the question of lost control. Even when contractors do military jobs, they remain private businesses and thus fall outside the military chain of command and justice systems. Unlike military units, PMFs retain a choice over which contracts they will take and can abandon or suspend operations for any reason, including if they become too dangerous or unprofitable; their employees, unlike soldiers, can always choose to walk off the job. Such freedom can leave the military in the lurch, as has occurred several times already in Iraq: during periods of intense violence, numerous private firms delayed, suspended, or ended their operations, placing great stress on U.S. troops. On other occasions, PMF employees endured even greater risks and dangers than their military equivalents. But military operations do not have room for such mixed results.

The Lack of Regulation

The second general challenge with PMFs stems from the unregulated nature of what has become a global industry. There are insufficient controls over who can work for these firms and for whom these firms can work. The recruiting, screening, and hiring of individuals for public military roles is left in private hands. In Iraq, this problem was magnified by the gold-rush effect: many firms entering the market were either entirely new to the business or had rapidly expanded. To be fair, many PMF employees are extremely well qualified. A great number of retired U.S. special forces operatives have served with PMFs in Iraq, as have former members of the United Kingdom's elite SAS (Special Air Service). But the rush for profits has led some corporations to cut corners in their screening procedures. For example, U.S. Army investigators of the Abu Ghraib prisoner-abuse scandal found that "approximately 35 percent of the contract interrogators [hired by the firm CACI] lacked formal military training as interrogators." In other cases, investigations of contractors serving in Iraq revealed the hiring of a former British Army soldier who had been jailed for working with Irish terrorists and a former South African soldier who had admitted to firebombing the houses of more than 60 political activists during the apartheid era.

Similar problems can occur with PMFs' clientele. Although military contractors have worked for democratic governments, the UN, and even humanitarian and environmental organizations, they have also been employed by dictatorships, rebel groups, drug cartels, and, prior to September 11, 2001, at least two al Qaeda-linked jihadi groups. A recent episode in Equatorial Guinea illustrates the problems that PMFs can run into in the absence of external guidance or rules. In March 2004, Logo Logistics, a British-South African PMF, was accused of plotting to overthrow the government in Malabo; a planeload of employees was arrested in Zimbabwe, and several alleged funders in the British aristocracy (including Sir Mark Thatcher, the son of Margaret Thatcher) were soon implicated in the scandal. The plotters have been accused of trying to topple Equatorial Guinea's government for profit motives. But their would-be victim, President Teodoro Obiang Nguema Mbasogo, is a corrupt dictator who took power by killing his uncle and runs one of the most despicable regimes on the continent—hardly a sympathetic victim.

War and Profits

In light of the fact that by now almost all of the factions of the ruling circles, including the White House and the neoconservative war-mongerers, acknowledge the failure of the Iraq War, why, then, do they balk at the idea of pulling the troops out of that country?

Perhaps the shortest path to a relatively satisfactory answer would be to follow the money trail. The fact of matter is that not everyone is losing in Iraq. Indeed, while the [George W.] Bush administration's wars of choice have brought unnecessary death, destruction, and disaster to millions, including many from the United States, they have also brought fortunes and prosperity to war profiteers. At the heart of the reluctance to withdraw from Iraq lies the profiteers' unwillingness to give up further fortunes and spoils of war.

Pentagon contractors constitute the overwhelming majority of these profiteers. They include not only the giant manufacturing contractors such as Lockheed Martin, Northrop Grumman and Boeing, but also a complex maze of over 100,000 service contractors and sub-contractors such as private army or security corporations and "reconstruction" firms. These contractors of both deconstruction and "reconstruction," whose profits come mainly from the US treasury, have handsomely profited from the Bush administration's wars of choice.

Ismael Hossein-zadeh,
"Why The U.S. Is Not Leaving Iraq:
The Booming Business of War Profiteers,"
Global Research, *January 12, 2007.*
www.globalresearch.ca.

Changing the Rules

The third concern raised by PMFs is, ironically, precisely the feature that makes them so popular with governments today: they can accomplish public ends through private means. In other words, they allow governments to carry out actions that would not otherwise be possible, such as those that would not gain legislative or public approval. Sometimes, such freedom is beneficial: it can allow countries to fill unrecognized or unpopular strategic needs. But it also disconnects the public from its foreign policy, removing certain activities from popular oversight.

The increased use of private contractors by the U.S. government in Colombia is one illustration of this trend: by hiring PMFs, the Bush administration has circumvented congressional limits on the size and scope of the U.S. military's involvement in Colombia's civil war. The use of PMFs in Iraq is another example: by privatizing parts of the U.S. mission, the Bush administration has dramatically lowered the political price for its Iraq policies. Were it not for the more than 20,000 contractors currently operating in the country, the U.S. government would have to either deploy more of its own troops there (which would mean either expanding the regular force or calling up more National Guard members and reservists) or persuade other countries to increase their commitments— either of which would require painful political compromises. By outsourcing parts of the job instead, the Bush administration has avoided such unappealing alternatives and has also been able to shield the full costs from scrutiny: contractor casualties and kidnappings are not listed on public rolls and are rarely mentioned by the media. PMF contracts are also not subject to Freedom of Information Act requests. This reduction in transparency raises deep concerns about the long-term health of American democracy. As the legal scholar Arthur S. Miller once wrote, "democratic government is responsible government—which means accountable government—and the essential problem in contracting out is that responsibility and accountability are greatly diminished."

Outside the Law

PMFs also create legal dilemmas, the fourth sort of policy challenge they raise. On both the personal and the corporate level, there is a striking absence of regulation, oversight, and enforcement. Although private military firms and their employees are now integral parts of many military operations, they tend to fall through the cracks of current legal codes, which sharply distinguish civilians from soldiers. Contractors are not quite civilians, given that they often carry and use weapons, interrogate prisoners, load bombs, and fulfill other critical military roles. Yet they are not quite soldiers, either. One military law analyst noted, "Legally speaking, [military contractors] fall into the same grey area as the unlawful combatants detained at Guantánamo Bay."

This lack of clarity means that when contractors are captured, their adversaries get to define their status. The results of this uncertainty can be dire—as they have been for three American employees of California Microwave Systems whose plane crashed in rebel-held territory in Colombia in 2003. The three have been held prisoner ever since, afforded none of the protections of the Geneva Conventions. Meanwhile, their corporate bosses and U.S. government clients seem to have washed their hands of the matter.

Such difficulties also play out when contractors commit misdeeds. It is often unclear how, when, where, and which authorities are responsible for investigating, prosecuting, and punishing such crimes. Unlike soldiers, who are accountable under their nation's military code of justice wherever they are located, contractors have a murky legal status, undefined by international law (they do not fit the formal definition of mercenaries). Normally, a civilian's crimes fall under the jurisdiction of the country where they are committed. But PMFs typically operate in failed states; indeed, the absence of local authority usually explains their presence in the first place. Prosecuting their crimes locally can thus be difficult.

Iraq, for example, still has no well-established courts, and during the formal U.S. occupation, regulations explicitly exempted contractors from local jurisdiction. Yet it is often just as difficult to prosecute contractors in their home country, since few legal systems cover crimes committed outside their territory. Some states do assert extraterritorial jurisdiction over their nationals, but they do so only for certain crimes and often lack the means to enforce their laws abroad. As a result of these gaps, not one private military contractor has been prosecuted or punished for a crime in Iraq (unlike the dozens of U.S. soldiers who have), despite the fact that more than 20,000 contractors have now spent almost two years there. Either every one of them happens to be a model citizen, or there are serious shortcomings in the legal system that governs them.

The failure to properly control the behavior of PMFs took on great consequence in the Abu Ghraib prisoner-abuse case. According to reports, all of the translators and up to half of the interrogators involved were private contractors working for two firms, Titan and CACI. The U.S. Army found that contractors were involved in 36 percent of the proven incidents and identified 6 employees as individually culpable. More than a year after the incidents, however, not one of these individuals has been indicted, prosecuted, or punished, even though the U.S. Army has found the time to try the enlisted soldiers involved. Nor has there been any attempt to assess corporate responsibility for the misdeeds. Indeed, the only formal inquiry into PMF wrongdoing on the corporate level was conducted by CACI itself. CACI investigated CACI and, unsurprisingly, found that CACI had done no wrong.

In the absence of legislation, some parties have already turned to litigation to address problems with PMFs—hardly the best forum for resolving issues related to human rights and the military. For example, some former Abu Ghraib prisoners have already tried to sue in U.S. courts the private firms involved with the prison. And the families of the four Blackwater employees murdered by insurgents in Fallujah have sued the company in a North Carolina court, claiming that the deceased had been sent into danger with a smaller unit than mandated in their contracts and with weapons, vehicles, and preparation that were not up to the standards promised.

Redefining the Public Military

The final dilemma raised by the extensive use of private contractors involves the future of the military itself. The armed services have long seen themselves as engaged in a unique profession, set apart from the rest of civilian society, which they are entrusted with securing. The introduction of PMFs, and their recruiting from within the military itself, challenges that uniqueness; the military's professional identity and monopoly on certain activities is being encroached on by the regular civilian marketplace. . . .

The forces that drove the growth of the private military industry seem set in place. Much like the Internet boom, the PMF bubble may burst if the current spate of work in Iraq ever ends, but the industry itself is unlikely to disappear anytime soon. Governments must therefore act to meet this reality. Using private solutions for public military ends is not necessarily a bad thing. But the stakes in warfare are far higher than in the corporate realm: in this most essential public sphere, national security and people's lives are constantly put at risk. War, as the old proverb has it, is certainly far too important to be left to the generals. The same holds true for the CEOs.

| "Tradition has its place, but let's not undermine vital military effectiveness with quaint concepts from the past."

Outsourcing Military Duties to Private Contractors Is Useful

Part I: Doug Brooks, Part II: Matan Chorev

In the following two viewpoints, both authors outline the ways in which the private military industry has been misunderstood and how outsourcing military duties to private companies has aided the military in accomplishing its missions. In the first viewpoint, Doug Brooks, president and founder of the International Peace Operations Association, a private military trade industry organization, argues that both political commentators and scholars have an archaic view of the role and status of militaries worldwide, which has in turn restricted implementation of policies that would improve the military's ability to carry out its missions. Brooks contends that the debate over what tasks should be performed only by government institutes ignores the ways in

Doug Brooks, "Part I: Who Is Really Burdening the Military? A Consideration of 'Inherently Governmental,'" *Journal of International Peace Operations*, vol. 4, July–August 2008, pp. 4, 28. Copyright © 2008 International Peace Operations Association. Reproduced by permission; Matan Chorev, "Part II: Comparing Apples to Oranges: Understanding the Diversity of the Peace and Stability Industry in Iraq," August 1, 2005. www.ipoaonline.org. Copyright © 2005 International Peace Operations Association. Reproduced by permission.

which advantages provided by outsourcing help the military operate at maximum effectiveness. In the second viewpoint, Harvard international affairs research assistant Matan Chorev addresses the specific roles filled by the private military industry in the Iraq conflict, and he sets out to concretely define the varying facets of the industry. Chorev maintains that precise definition of the industry and its operations will lead to increased productivity and ultimately limit the duration of military operations overseas.

As you read, consider the following questions:

1. According to Brooks, how is the military different than pundits' and academics' nineteenth-century understanding of the institution?

2. What four reasons does Chorev give to demonstrate how delineation of the private military industry into "different service components" would be beneficial?

3. What are the three types of private military service providers, and what are the differences among their services, according to Chorev?

Part I

One of the more important current discussions is the issue of 'inherently governmental,' a concept that has momentous repercussions for international security policy in Iraq and around the world. In the United States this term refers to which responsibilities can be entrusted to the private sector and which are best assigned only to government employees. Unfortunately, the debate turns largely around the question of what is traditionally governmental rather than what must be governmental, and this concept has enormous implications for global military and stability operations. Perhaps even more ominous, the discussion is closely intertwined with the emotional debate on the Iraq conflict, making rational decisions ever more difficult.

A New Definition of the Military

Western militaries in the 21st century are becoming smaller, more professional, more capable and smarter than in the past, yet too many pundits and academics are mired in a 19th-century understanding of a military: the archaic concept of mass militaries with hapless soldiers ordered to do everything from potato-peeling to gate-guarding to ditch-digging. Strident advocacy of this anachronistic notion has been undermining military reforms toward effectiveness and efficiency. Demands that militaries return to the old concept undermines the ability of the international community to implement national and international goals and policies, not just in controversial conflicts such as Afghanistan and Iraq, but in humanitarian operations where everyone would like to see success, such as Darfur and Eastern Democratic Republic of Congo.

I often make the point that U.S. operations in Afghanistan and Iraq are the best supported and best supplied military operations in history. This observation is based not just on my own visits to these countries, but by numerous soldiers' accounts, and even by some critics of privatization who have cringed at the comforts provided to modern soldiers. This level of support is a direct result of inspired utilization of the private sector to build and support bases, transport personnel and supplies, reconstruct infrastructure and even provide private security—largely by locals—for much of the perimeter and convoy security duties. These services certainly cannot guarantee success, but they do allow a relatively limited military force to better focus on its core missions.

Improving Regulation

For the U.S. government, a great deal can be done to improve the way in which the military uses and oversees contractors—improved oversight is far more beneficial to the mission than the current congressional trend towards post-contract audits. IPOA [International Peace Operations Association] member

Beyond Petty Political Concerns

The private sector brings enormous surge capacities and specialized capabilities to international peace operations. Private companies are increasingly recognized for their ability to operate in highly volatile environments faster, better, and more cost-effectively than can more traditional actors such as UN [United Nations] peacekeeping forces or the U.S. military. They can do this because they are able to draw upon the most capable personnel not just from a single country, but from the entire world, and because they are far less likely to be hampered by the bureaucratic and petty political concerns that hinder the decision-making processes of governments and large international organizations.

Derek Wright, "The Critical Role of the Private Sector in International Peace and Stability Operations," Humanitarian Development Summit, *October 3, 2006.*

companies working with the U.S. government have been vocal in their criticisms of government oversight in Afghanistan and Iraq (although there has been gradual improvement). Good oversight also makes it easier for contractors to do their jobs since contracts in post-conflict environments often need modifications to adapt to evolving risk levels and address political complexities. Just as importantly, companies carefully following the thousands of rules and regulations, putting money and effort into compliance, and ensuring that they are accomplishing their tasks as required deserve credit. Those companies which fail to follow the rules must be identified and sanctioned. Steve Schooner of the George Washington University Law School has been a vocal proponent of reforming oversight, and the recent U.S. Army report produced by the Gansler Commission has made numerous practical suggestions on how contracting oversight must be improved. This improvement will not be instantaneous or perfect, but the process should not be allowed to distract from the phenomenal value of the basic model of private support for international polices.

We should not be harking back to the 19th century; we should not be trying to burden already overtaxed soldiers with work that the private sector can accomplish better and more cost-effectively. The 21st century promises more peace and stability operations in more places and we will need professional militaries more than ever. Tradition has its place, but let's not undermine vital military effectiveness with quaint concepts from the past.

Part II

An apple is a fruit. So is an orange. Comparing the two, however, is all too often a fruitless endeavor. Nonetheless, some seem intent on doing just that when it comes to private contractors in Iraq.

If we are to get a handle on the myriad of difficult ethical and operational questions regarding the increasing role of private contractors in Iraq, we must commit to developing a nuanced understanding of the diversity of services offered by the peace and stability industry. Unfortunately, overly simplistic portrayals of the industry have thwarted progress in the public dialogue on privatization. Detractors of the so-called "privatization of national security" label the industry as a "coalition of the billing" who profit from the continuance of instability and suffering in Iraq. Advocates of privatization see the industry as filling the supply-demand gap for peacekeeping, providing logistical and support functions and other services in conflict/post-conflict zones.

Defining a Complex and Varied Industry

The fact is that the industry is multifaceted. Delineation of the industry into its different service components is helpful from a conceptual standpoint for both the government and the industry for four reasons. First, it will assist the shared goal of refining regulatory mechanisms to address only those companies to which they should be made applicable. Second, the government will become a better client in that it will be more aware of what it is purchasing and more capable of relaying that information to taxpayers in a transparent manner. Third, understanding the fine distinctions of the private sector will allow for more thorough and meaningful assessments of its field implications. Finally, such review will improve war planning, as it will be easier to figure out when and under what conditions outsourcing to the private sector is appropriate and cost effective.

The industry is essentially made up of three major types of service providers—Nonlethal Service Providers (NSPs), Private Security Companies (PSCs), and Private Military Companies (PMCs). Companies that provide logistics, transportation, or supply fall under the category of NSPs. In contrast, PSCs work to protect industrial and government sites, convoys, and government officials, and also provide humanitarian aid protection. Lastly, PMCs are contracted by states to provide military services, from the training of military and police forces to organizational issues that can alter the strategic reality of a conflict environment.

Cleaning latrines and cooking meals is a vastly different task than guarding the head of the Provisional Coalition Authority (CPA) in Iraq, but both act as crucial force multipliers that allow the military to focus on what it does best—fight the insurgency. It does a great disservice to the industry and to consumers of news when reports do not clarify the service provisions of these companies.

Clarifying the Industry's Role Through Policy Reform

Like any sector, different components of the industry at times find themselves working in parallel or using the services of one another. Subsidiary companies and subcontracting complicate the design of regulatory mechanisms. However, these practices do not make oversight impossible to achieve. Many companies have united to ask for clearer laws and increased regulation. For example, the International Peace Operations Association (IPOA), a trade association of private contractors working in conflict/post-conflict environments, has been working for greater transparency and accountability. Our elected officials must continue to demonstrate leadership and push additional legislation forward. Nevertheless, private contractors should be encouraged to clarify their service role.

The diversity of services in the industry is not new. What is new, is the sheer volume of actors and the increased reliance on the private sector to assist in the different facets of military life. It is therefore all the more pressing to put forth an effort to make the industry more effective and accountable. A sober dialogue divorced from pundit-driven analysis is long overdue. A sophisticated understanding of the service provisions is an important first step to yielding a safer, more effective, accountable, and ultimately successful operation that will spare the lives of coalition forces, civilians, and the Iraqi people while ultimately minimizing the length of the U.S. presence in Iraq.

> "There is no way for the American public ... to know how those contractors are getting the money, what they are doing with it, or how effectively they are using it."

Outsourcing Intelligence Jobs to the Private Sector Does Not Benefit the Public

Tim Shorrock

Tim Shorrock contends in the following viewpoint that the outsourcing of government intelligence duties, traditionally performed by the Central Intelligence Agency (CIA) and other government agencies, to private companies creates a situation in which accountability is limited and corruption is possible. He argues that the often secretive nature of the contracts is the root of many potential problems. Further, Shorrock states that the private intelligence contractors and their lobbyists have access to classified documents that public lobbyists cannot access, giving contractors an advantage in advocating policies economically favorable to them. Tim Shorrock is an investigative reporter whose articles on foreign policy and other government issues have ap-

Tim Shorrock, "The Corporate Takeover of U.S. Intelligence," *Salon*, June 1, 2007. www.salon.com. This article first appeared in Salon.com, at http://www.salon.com. An online version remains in the Salon archives. Reprinted with permission.

peared in numerous publications. He is also the author of the book Spies for Hire: The Secret World of Intelligence Outsourcing.

As you read, consider the following questions:

1. Figures from the Office of the Director of National Intelligence show that intelligence contracts increased by how much from 1995 to 2005?

2. According to the author, what are some examples of jobs and tasks once performed only by government employees but are now carried out by private sector employees?

3. According to Shorrock, what percentage of intelligence contracts are classified, making their budgets secret?

More than five years into the global "war on terror," spying has become one of the fastest-growing private industries in the United States. The federal government relies more than ever on outsourcing for some of its most sensitive work, though it has kept details about its use of private contractors a closely guarded secret. Intelligence experts, and even the government itself, have warned of a critical lack of oversight for the booming intelligence business.

On May 14 [2007], at an industry conference in Colorado sponsored by the Defense Intelligence Agency, the U.S. government revealed for the first time how much of its classified intelligence budget is spent on private contracts: a whopping 70 percent.

The DNI [office of the Director of National Intelligence] figures show that the aggregate number of private contracts awarded by intelligence agencies rose by about 38 percent from the mid-1990s to 2005. But the surge in outsourcing has been far more dramatic measured in dollars: Over the same period of time, the total value of intelligence contracts more than doubled, from about $18 billion in 1995 to about $42 billion in 2005.

"Those numbers are startling," said Steven Aftergood, the director of the Project on Government Secrecy at the Federation of American Scientists and an expert on the U.S. intelligence budget. "They represent a transformation of the Cold War intelligence bureaucracy into something new and different that is literally dominated by contractor interests."

The Lack of Transparency

Because of the cloak of secrecy thrown over the intelligence budgets, there is no way for the American public, or even much of Congress, to know how those contractors are getting the money, what they are doing with it, or how effectively they are using it. The explosion in outsourcing has taken place against a backdrop of intelligence failures for which the [George W.] Bush administration has been hammered by critics, from Saddam Hussein's fictional weapons of mass destruction to abusive interrogations that have involved employees of private contractors operating in Iraq, Afghanistan and Guantánamo Bay, Cuba. Aftergood and other experts also warn that the lack of transparency creates conditions ripe for corruption.

Trey Brown, a DNI press officer, told *Salon* that the 70 percent figure disclosed by Everett refers to everything that U.S. intelligence agencies buy, from pencils to buildings to "whatever devices we use to collect intelligence." Asked how much of the money doled out goes toward big-ticket items like military spy satellites, he replied, "We can't really talk about those kinds of things."

The media has reported on some contracting figures for individual agencies, but never before for the entire U.S. intelligence enterprise. In 2006, the *Washington Post* reported that a "significant majority" of the employees at two key agencies, the National Counterterrorism Center and the Pentagon's Counter-Intelligence Field Activity [CIFA] office, were contractors (at CIFA, the number was more than 70 percent).

More recently, former officers with the Central Intelligence Agency [CIA] have said the CIA's workforce is about 60 percent contractors.

Public Jobs Performed by Private Companies

But the statistics alone don't even show the degree to which outsourcing has penetrated U.S. intelligence—many tasks and services once reserved exclusively for government employees are being handled by civilians. For example, private contractors analyze much of the intelligence collected by satellites and low-flying unmanned aerial vehicles, and they write reports that are passed up to the line to high-ranking government officials. They supply and maintain software programs that can manipulate and depict data used to track terrorist suspects, both at home and abroad, and determine what targets to hit in hot spots in Iraq and Afghanistan. Such data is also at the heart of the National Security Agency's [NSA] massive eavesdropping programs and may be one reason the DNI is pushing Congress to grant immunity to corporations that may have cooperated with the NSA over the past five years. Contractors also provide collaboration tools to help individual agencies communicate with each other, and they supply security tools to protect intelligence networks from outside tampering.

Outsourcing has also spread into the realm of human intelligence. At the CIA, contractors help staff overseas stations and provide disguises used by agents working undercover. According to Robert Baer, the former CIA officer who was the inspiration for the character played by George Clooney in the film *Syriana*, a contractor stationed in Iraq even supervises where CIA agents go in Baghdad and whom they meet. "It's a completely different culture from the way the CIA used to be run, when a case officer determined where and when agents would go," he told me in a recent interview. "Everyone I know in the CIA is leaving and going into contracting whether they're retired or not."

Questions About the Effectiveness of Outsourcing

The DNI itself has voiced doubts about the efficiency and effectiveness of outsourcing. In a public report released ... fall [2006], the agency said the intelligence community increasingly "finds itself in competition with its contractors for our own employees." Faced with arbitrary staffing limits and uncertain funding, the report said, intelligence agencies are forced "to use contractors for work that may be borderline 'inherently governmental'"—meaning the agencies have no clear idea about what work should remain exclusively inside the government versus work that can be done by civilians working for private firms. The DNI also found that "those same contractors recruit our own employees, already cleared and trained at government expense, and then 'lease' them back to us at considerably greater expense."

A Senate Intelligence Committee report ... spells out the costs to taxpayers. It estimates that the average annual cost for a government intelligence officer is $126,500, compared to the average $250,000 (including overhead) paid by the government for an intelligence contractor. "Given this cost disparity," the report concluded, "the Committee believes that the Intelligence Community [IC] should strive in the long term to reduce its dependence upon contractors."

The DNI began an intensive study of contracting ... [in 2006], but when its "IC Core Contractor Inventory" report was sent to Congress ..., DNI officials refused to release its findings to the public, citing risks to national security. The next month, a report from the House Permanent Select Committee on Intelligence rebuked the DNI in unusually strong language, concluding that U.S. officials "do not have an adequate understanding of the size and composition of the contractor work force, a consistent and well-articulated method for assessing contractor performance, or strategies for managing a combined staff-contractor workforce."

U.S. intelligence budgets are classified, and all discussions about them in Congress are held in secret. Much of the information, however, is available to intelligence contractors, who are at liberty to lobby members of Congress about the budgets, potentially skewing policy in favor of the contractors. For example, Science Applications International Corp., one of the nation's largest intelligence contractors, spent $1,330,000 in their congressional lobbying efforts in 2006, which included a focus on the intelligence and defense budgets, according to records filed with the Senate's Office of Public Records.

The public, of course, is completely excluded from these discussions. "It's not like a debate when someone loses," said Aftergood. "There *is* no debate. And the more work that migrates to the private sector, the less effective congressional oversight is going to be." From that secretive process, he added, "there's only a short distance to the Duke Cunninghams of the world and the corruption of the process in the interest of private corporations." In March 2006, Randy "Duke" Cunningham, R[epublican]-Calif., who had resigned from Congress several months earlier, was sentenced to eight years in prison after being convicted of accepting more than $2 million in bribes from executives with MZM, a prominent San Diego defense contractor. In return for the bribes, Cunningham used his position on the House appropriations and intelligence committees to win tens of millions of dollars' worth of contracts for MZM at the CIA and the Pentagon's CIFA office, which has been criticized by Congress for spying on American citizens. The MZM case deepened ... when Kyle "Dusty" Foggo, the former deputy director of the CIA, was indicted for conspiring with former MZM CEO Brent Wilkes to steer contracts toward the company.

The Private Sector Developments
Surpass the Public Ones

U.S. intelligence agencies have always relied on private companies for technology and hardware. Lockheed built the famous U-2 spy plane under specifications from the CIA, and dozens of companies, from TRW to Polaroid to Raytheon, helped develop the high-resolution cameras and satellites that beamed information back to Washington about the Soviet Union and its military and missile installations. The National Security Agency, which was founded in the early 1950s to monitor foreign communications and telephone calls, hired IBM, Cray and other companies to make the supercomputers that helped the agency break encryption codes and transform millions of bits of data into meaningful intelligence.

By the 1990s, however, commercial developments in encryption, information technology, imagery and satellites had outpaced the government's ability to keep up, and intelligence agencies began to turn to the private sector for technologies they once made in-house. Agencies also turned to outsourcing after Congress, as part of the "peace dividend" that followed the end of the Cold War, cut defense and intelligence budgets by about 30 percent.

When the National Geospatial-Intelligence Agency [NGA] was created in 1995 as the primary collection agency for imagery and mapping, for example, it immediately began buying its software and much of its satellite imagery from commercial vendors; today, half of its 14,000 workers are full-time equivalent contractors who work inside NGA facilities but collect their paychecks from companies like Booz Allen Hamilton and Lockheed Martin. In the late 1990s, the NSA began outsourcing its internal telecommunications and even some of its signals analysis to private companies, such as Computer Services Corp. and SAIC.

CIA Contractor's Marketing Reveals Sensitive Intelligence Information

US national security is compromised by the Intelligence Community's heavy dependence upon corporations, corporations whose Web sites sometimes spill out some of the darkest government secrets to those who know how to read them. [February 2008] revelations by D/CIA [Director of the Central Intelligence Agency, General Michael V.] Hayden that CIA contractors have been involved in enhanced interrogation techniques at detention facilities (i.e. waterboarding at black sites) should make it clear even to the casual observer that private corporations are integrally involved in the Intelligence Community's most sensitive and secretive clandestine and covert programs. Nothing is off-limits. Corporate involvement in clandestine programs raises operational security concerns that only exist because these companies market their services to the private sector, capitalizing upon their exotic experience with the US government.

In other words, we're taking risks with our national security, risks we don't have to take. Perhaps some of the risk can be mitigated through restrictions upon contractor marketing and better contractor policing. As a big fan of the private sector and of government outsourcing, I don't like to think that the problem is inherent to outsourcing, but at the moment, it's hard to imagine it otherwise.

R.J. Hillhouse, "Contractor's Website Reveals Clandestine CIA Programs," The Spy Who Billed Me, February 19, 2008. www.thespywhobilledme.com.

The Impact of the 9/11 Terrorist Attacks

Outsourcing increased dramatically after 9/11 [2001]. The Bush administration and Congress, determined to prevent further terrorist attacks, ordered a major increase in intelligence spending and organized new institutions to fight the war on terror, such as the National Counterterrorism Center. To beef up these organizations, the CIA and other agencies were authorized to hire thousands of analysts and human intelligence specialists. Partly because of the big cuts of the 1990s, however, many of the people with the skills and security clearances to do that work were working in the private sector. As a result, contracting grew quickly as intelligence agencies rushed to fill the gap.

That increase can be seen in the DNI documents showing contract award dollars: Contract spending, based on the DNI data and estimates from this period, remained fairly steady from 1995 to 2001, at about $20 billion a year. In 2002, the first year after the attacks on New York and Washington, contracts jumped to about $32 billion. In 2003 they jumped again, reaching about $42 billion. They have remained steady since then through 2006 (the DNI data is current as of . . . August [2006]).

Because nearly 90 percent of intelligence contracts are classified and the budgets kept secret, it's difficult to draw up a list of top contractors and their revenues derived from intelligence work. Based on publicly available information, including filings from publicly traded companies with the Securities and Exchange Commission and company press releases and Web sites, the current top five intelligence contractors appear to be Lockheed Martin, Northrop Grumman, SAIC, General Dynamics and L-3 Communications. Other major contractors include Booz Allen Hamilton, CACI International, DRS Technologies and Mantech International. The industry's growth and dependence on government budgets has made intelligence contracting an attractive market for former high-ranking national security officials, like former CIA director George Tenet, who now earns millions of dollars working as a director and advisor to four companies that hold contracts with U.S. intelligence agencies and do big business in Iraq and elsewhere.

Removing the Cloak of Secrecy

Congress, meanwhile, is beginning to ask serious questions about intelligence outsourcing and how lawmakers influence the intelligence budget process. Some of that interest has been generated by the Cunningham scandal. In another recent case, Rep. Rick Renzi, a Republican from Arizona, resigned from the House Intelligence Committee in April [2007] because he is under federal investigation for introducing legislation that may have benefited Mantech International, a major intelligence contractor where Renzi's father works in a senior executive position.

In the Cunningham case, many of MZM's illegal contracts were funded by "earmarks" that he inserted in intelligence bills. Earmarks, typically budget items placed by lawmakers to benefit projects or companies in their district, are often difficult to find amid the dense verbiage of legislation—and in the "black" intelligence budgets, they are even harder to find. In its recent budget report, the House Intelligence Committee listed 26 separate earmarks for intelligence contracts, along with the sponsor's name and the dollar amount of the contract. The names of the contractors, however, were not included in the list.

Both the House and Senate are now considering intelligence spending bills that require the DNI, starting [in 2008] . . . , to provide extensive information on contractors. The House version requires an annual report on contractors that might be committing waste and fraud, as well as reviews on its "accountability mechanisms" for contractors and the effect of contractors on the intelligence workforce. The amendment was drafted by Rep. David Price, D[emocrat]-N.C., who introduced a similar bill . . . that passed the House but was quashed by the Senate. In a statement on the House floor . . . , Price explained that he was seeking answers to several simple questions: "Should (contractors) be involved in intelligence collection? Should they be involved in analysis? What about interrogations or covert operations? Are there some activities that are *so* sensitive they should only be performed by highly trained Intelligence Community professionals?"

If either of the House or Senate intelligence bills pass in their present form, the overall U.S. intelligence budget will be made public. Such transparency is critical as contracting continues to expand, said Paul Cox, Price's press secretary. "As a nation," he said, "we really need to take a look and decide what's appropriate to contract and what's inherently governmental."

> *"The CIA does have many good analysts, but the organizational prioritization of group-think and seniority strangles them."*

Outsourcing Intelligence Jobs to the Private Sector Would Benefit the Public

Michael Rubin

In the following viewpoint, Michael Rubin explains how doling out many functions of the Central Intelligence Agency (CIA) to private intelligence firms would improve the collection and analysis of data, in turn increasing U.S. national security. He outlines how problems within both the CIA and the Federal Bureau of Investigation (FBI) have contributed to intelligence failures in the past and argues that privatization would ensure that the same mistakes are not made again. Michael Rubin served as a staff advisor on Iraq and Iran within the Office of the Secretary of Defense from 2002 to 2004 and is currently a resident scholar at the American Enterprise Institute.

Michael Rubin, "Privatize the CIA: Our Intelligence Community Could Use More Competition," *Weekly Standard*, vol. 12, February 5, 2007. Copyright © 2007 News Corporation, Weekly Standard. All rights reserved. Reproduced by permission.

As you read, consider the following questions:

1. What reasons does the author give to explain the poor analysis produced by the CIA?
2. What are the benefits of privatization in the intelligence community, as explained by Rubin?
3. How could the government mitigate the risks of privatization, according to the author?

On January 23 and 25, [2007,] the Senate Select Committee on Intelligence held hearings on intelligence reform. Topics included the remaining 9/11 Commission [an investigation set up in 2002 to recount and respond to the terrorist attacks of 2001] recommendations and efforts both to facilitate information-sharing across the U.S. government's 16 intelligence agencies and to increase the number of operatives and linguists.

The committee's schedule suggests [Democratic] Sen. Jay Rockefeller [from West Virginia] will use his new majority status and chairmanship to increase oversight and press the [George W.] Bush administration on matters ranging from CIA rendition programs to the National Security Agency's warrantless surveillance programs. Oversight should be welcome, but neither it nor the 9/11 Commission's recommendations will be enough to rectify the quality of U.S. intelligence analysis.

Bureaucratic Hiring Problems

In a seminal article in the *Economist* in 1955, historian C. Northcote Parkinson described the behavior of bureaucracies. First, he observed, any "official wants to multiply subordinates, not rivals; and [second,] officials make work for each other." He used the British admiralty to illustrate his case. Between 1914 and 1928, its commissioned ships declined two-thirds. Over the same period of time, the number of officials managing them almost doubled.

As John Negroponte [appointed Deputy Secretary of State in February 2007] prepares to move from the directorship of National Intelligence to Foggy Bottom [the Washington, D.C., neighborhood where the U.S. Department of Justice is located], it is clear that his legacy falls far short of real reform. He hired 1,500 employees for his new office, but missed recruitment targets for both operatives and analysts.

This is failure. As both the Iranian nuclear drive and al Qaeda's declared war on the United States continue, the nation needs spies to peer where satellites cannot and men on the ground to hear conversations that take place in caves rather than on cell phones. The failure to recruit and retain quality linguists is also a scandal. While Rockefeller criticizes wiretap procedures, the true outrage is the failure of the intelligence and law enforcement communities to put the products of such surveillance to use. On July 27, 2005, Glenn Fine, inspector general for the U.S. Department of Justice, testified before the Senate Judiciary Committee that the Federal Bureau of Investigation backlog of counterterrorism and counterintelligence audio surveillance awaiting translation had grown from almost 25,000 hours on December 31, 2003, to more than 38,000 hours on March 31, 2005. Department of Justice sources say the problem has not diminished.

While the number of spies and linguists may be a critical metric for gauging U.S. capabilities, access to raw material does not itself correlate with quality analysis. Here, the intelligence community falls short. Take Larry Johnson, a former CIA and State Department analyst to whom the CIA awarded two Exceptional Performance commendations. On July 10, 2001, Johnson penned a *New York Times* op-ed entitled "The Declining Terrorist Threat." As Mohamed Atta and the other 9/11 hijackers conducted dry runs for their attack, and despite Osama bin Laden's 1998 declaration of war on the United States, Johnson argued that Americans were not primary targets of terrorism. He blamed concern about Islamist terrorism on "24-hour broadcast news operations too eager to find a dramatic story line."

While Johnson is just one public example, the poor quality of the CIA's analytical products is an open secret among intelligence consumers. Reports circulated to the State Department, Pentagon, Treasury Department, National Security Council, and the White House are seldom more analytical or detailed than published newspaper accounts.

Multiple Explanations for Poor Analysis

The reasons for poor analysis are multifold. The initial premise of a closed analytical shop segregated from policy was to maintain a bank of first-rate social scientists to prevent surprise and predict events. But social science has never lived up to its promise. The Soviet Union's collapse and 9/11 are just two prominent instances of the CIA's failure to predict. While it has become fashionable to scapegoat Iraqi National Congress head Ahmad Chalabi for faulty intelligence about Iraqi weapons, and thereby exculpate the CIA's perhaps $30 billion intelligence operation, the preponderance of Langley's [a town in Virginia, home to CIA headquarters and used here as a metonym for the CIA] analysis suggested Iraq was permeated with chemical and biological munitions.

Nor did Langley ever attract top academics. Many specialists shy away from government careers. In practice—unbelievable as it may seem—travel and regional experience disqualify applicants during the security clearance process. Those with native fluency in languages like Arabic, Persian, or Pashtun seldom pass CIA vetting. While Langley recruits Mormons returning from missions with linguistic ability, most intelligence hires are book smart but experience poor.

As a result, the products of the intelligence community lack both cultural nuance and a feel for personalities. Too many analysts assume that Iranian officials approach diplomacy with the sincerity of their U.S. counterparts; they cannot imagine the prospect that seminary-trained clerics practice religiously sanctioned dissimulation. Hence, many intelligence professionals at the time believed that Iranian president Mohammad Khatami was sincere in his calls for a dialogue of civilizations; now it is apparent that he pursued Iran's covert nuclear program with the same energy as his successor. When European leaders and Secretary of State Madeleine Albright relaxed sanctions and offered an olive branch to Tehran [the capital of Iran], the Islamic Republic used the resulting hard currency influx to upgrade Iran's military and fuel its covert nuclear program.

Cubicle isolation is also apparent to anyone who knows the people about whom dossiers are compiled. When writing biographies of Iraqi politicians, CIA analysts commonly erred on such basic information as the languages they spoke, let alone their predilections or personalities.

Extreme compartmentalization also reduces the chances for sound comparative analysis. As the CIA has grown, its analysts' areas of responsibility have narrowed. Expertise in arcane subjects should be welcome, but if it comes at the expense of comparative analysis, much can be lost. Analysis of Iranian nuclear capabilities, for example, should not be separated from study of the North Korean ballistic missile program or Pakistani weapons design. Nor should Iran area specialists be segregated from al Qaeda analysts. Rogue regimes and terrorists do not always compartmentalize relationships as neatly as does the U.S. bureaucracy.

The Lack of Accountability

The CIA does have many good analysts, but the organizational prioritization of group-think and seniority strangles them. Bureaucratic interests dominate. As reports filter up through multiple levels, officials insert trap-door statements to assert the opposite of any conclusion so that if the report's thrust is wrong, the agency can be absolved of responsibility. A single sentence questioning Saddam's weapons programs, for example, might be buried on page 17 of a report otherwise declaring their existence.

As former CIA operative Reuel Marc Gerecht points out, the formulaic assumption that any watershed event is five-to-ten years away is both the product of caution and a way to avoid acknowledging ignorance. Repeated statements that Iran is five-to-ten years away from autonomous nuclear capability, for example, have become the 21st-century equivalent of the Ten-Year Rule that left Great Britain scrambling to meet the challenge of a resurgent Germany prior to World War II.

Secrecy protects shoddy analysis. Langley may oust analysts for security reasons, but, like any government body, it seldom purges mediocrity. While intelligence analysts conflate questioning with politicization, the desire to avoid inquiry is often a sign of lack of confidence. Analysts who publish openly and under their own names must, for the sake of their reputations, produce solid work or else they will hemorrhage credibility and jeopardize their employment. Too often, though, intelligence briefers cannot answer basic questions. When queries are followed by requests to see raw intelligence, the source material does not always support the proffered conclusions. Intelligence professionals should be able and willing to defend their products.

It is this phenomenon that was at the root of tension between the CIA's Directorate of Intelligence and the Defense Department's Iraq policy shop. The forthcoming report of an investigation by the Pentagon's Office of Inspector General into the Office of Special Plans will absolve the unit of charges that it produced its own intelligence—it did not—but the report may criticize the office for questioning too much the products it received from Langley. But to move toward a standard of blind acceptance of intelligence would be both dangerous and wrong.

A History of Outsourced Intelligence Gathering

Despite increased public attention focused on the practice of "outsourcing" intelligence support functions, this phenomenon is certainly not unprecedented. Indeed, it was not until the early 20th century that the United States possessed a professionally trained, organic intelligence capability within the government. Prior to that time military intelligence was largely an improvised affair, conducted by cavalry scouts and managed by line officers with no formal intelligence training. Due to the lack of dedicated personnel, the collection and analysis of intelligence information was often delegated to civilian auxiliaries employed on short-term assignments for specified tasks. In many respects, the current system of ad hoc commercial augmentation is similar to the earliest practices used by the military to satisfy short-term intelligence needs.

During the American Revolution the absence of a professional intelligence staff required augmentation by civilian spy networks to supplement military reconnaissance. It is estimated that General [George] Washington spent more than 10 percent of his wartime expenditures on intelligence related activities, much of this funding to support civilian agents collecting critical information on British operations. . . .

Following the war most of the army's intelligence functions were informally delegated to topographic engineers, signal officers, or cavalry scouts, but throughout the 19th century regular army assets were frequently supplemented by non-military specialists to provide unique skills or expertise. One such example from the Mexican-American War was the so-called "Mexican Spy Company," a quasi-military force contracted by American commanders to provide local intelligence, counter-espionage services, surveillance, and route reconnaissance in support of U.S. forces.

Glen James Voelz, "Managing the Private Spies:
The Use of Commercial Augmentation for Intelligence Operations,"
Center for Strategic Intelligence Research,
Discussion Paper Number Fourteen, June 2006.

The traditional value of intelligence products was to provide a baseline of neutral expertise, but the era of an apolitical Langley is over. In November 2005, W. Patrick Lang, former defense intelligence officer for the Middle East, South Asia, and counterterrorism, told the *American Prospect* of CIA analysts' attempts to hurt the White House prior to the 2004 election. "Of course they were leaking," he said. "They told me about it at the time. They thought it was funny. They'd say things like, 'This last thing that came out, surely people will pay attention to that. They won't reelect this man [President Bush].'" Intelligence analysts should not participate in policy making. Their frequent and as-yet-unplugged leaks may win some short-term policy battles for Langley, but such illegalities have badly damaged trust. To suggest the Directorate of Intelligence is policy-neutral is risible.

Benefits of Working Outside the Government

So what is the solution? Washington's inclination is always to expand hiring. But that will constrain rather than improve analysis. Today, the CIA's analytical wing is the ultimate expression of Parkinson's Law, rather than a generator of accurate explanation or prediction. Rather than expand, the government should privatize much of its analysis.

Privatization works. Already, Beltway firms like SAIC and Booz Allen Hamilton operate streamlined intelligence shops. Their analysts hold the highest security clearances. So do many think-tank scholars and some university academics. Many private-sector analysts have language abilities and experience their government counterparts lack.

Freeing analysts from some government rules and regulations could improve their products. Not only would it enable outside-of-the-box thinking, but it could also improve access. U.S. government personnel visiting Beirut, let alone Baghdad, must adhere to embassy regulations stipulating intrusive security for travel outside compound walls. Nongovernment employees roam free—or at least set their own rules for security.

Privatization would improve productivity. It can take the CIA hierarchy weeks to sign off on an analyst's report and release it to intelligence consumers across the U.S. government. Private companies react faster. Competition might also expedite exploitation of several million pages of documents seized in Afghanistan and Iraq.

A decade ago, the CIA curtailed its subscriber-based circulation of foreign newspapers and media broadcasts in translation, partly for financial reasons and partly out of misdirected hand-wringing that such products might violate even North Korean and Iranian intellectual property rights. Today, the Open Source Center, the office within the CIA that translates published material, still withholds much of its product from the public. Getting this into the hands of a wider pool of analysts would be in the national interest, even if the analysts offered differing interpretations.

Expanding the pool of professionals who hold security clearances would have auxiliary benefit. Not only would it enable more opinion and debate without the costs of salary and pension; but, in the long term, it would also erode the clearance lag. Even with "expedite" orders, whoever wins the presidency in 2008 will have to wait 15 months to staff the National Security Council with new faces unless they already hold clearances. At present, the CIA spends hundreds of thousands of dollars to screen and train analysts who may leave government service after only a couple of years. Making it easier for the U.S. government to employ such people would increase return on investment.

Privatization for Protection

There would be drawbacks to more privatization—security and counterintelligence problems would expand—but the risks need not be excessive. Even State Department student interns receive top-secret clearances. Access to government products should still require background checks, security clearance, and the incumbent oaths to protect the material. The FBI and other relevant agencies should nevertheless expand counterintelligence checks. Dissemination of sensitive compartmentalized information like signals and communications intercepts should, of course, remain subject to the presence of adequate facilities to handle and protect the information.

Some outside scholars might also cherry-pick data. But then government intelligence analysts do so now. While data are open to interpretation, competition exposes bad methodology, and ultimately quality shines through. Individual authorship promotes accountability.

Would the CIA's analytical wing disappear? No. But it should shrink, as the pool of outside experts expands. Much of the money allocated for the analytical wing would be better applied to the Directorates of Operations and Science & Technology. Langley and its consumers might maintain yellow pages of analysts by expertise and repositories of finished products. Congressmen could call on individuals to explain their reports or even have multiple specialists debate interpretations. It is not uncommon in, say, the Pentagon for senior leaders to host closed debates among academics and analysts. One thing is certain, though. With threats multiplying, bloat and a culture of job security over performance will neither protect the United States nor promote the serious thinking needed to help it face new challenges.

> *"Existing policy draws a sharp distinction between close allies—allies such as Britain—and most of the world's other countries when it comes to vigilance against possible terrorism."*

Outsourcing U.S. Port Operation Is a National Security Risk

Michael E. O'Hanlon

In the following viewpoint, Michael E. O'Hanlon contends that while United Arab Emirates (UAE) is a highly regarded ally in the fight against terrorism, the outsourcing of port operations to a UAE corporation could pose potential risks to U.S. security now and in the future. O'Hanlon argues that it is prudent to be cautious and recognize the difference between long-time U.S. allies, such as Britain, and those more recently formed relationships with countries such as UAE. He also outlines specific characteristics of UAE that make operation of U.S. ports by one of its companies problematic. Michael E. O'Hanlon is a Brookings Institution senior fellow specializing in issues relating to U.S. national security policy.

Michael E. O'Hanlon, "Port Deal Raises Serious Concerns," *Baltimore Sun*, March 2, 2006. Reproduced by permission of the author.

As you read, consider the following questions:

1. What are some of the behaviors in United Arab Emirates' "not-too-distant past" that O'Hanlon mentions to support his advocacy of caution?

2. What are the qualities that our close allies possess that most other countries do not, according to O'Hanlon?

3. What three areas does the author believe deserve further investigation before any final decision on the UAE ports operation deal is reached?

Judging by the recent [2006] statements of its top officials, the [George W.] Bush administration intends to use the 45-day investigation period for the proposed Dubai Ports World [DPW] transaction simply to let nerves calm and emotions cool in the hope that Congress and key state officials will then accept the deal. This perspective is unfortunate.

Real issues need to be addressed if a company owned and operated by the United Arab Emirates [UAE] is to safely manage key operations at six U.S. ports. The opposition to the deal of former 9/11 commissioner[1] Thomas H. Kean, a former governor of New Jersey, and at least one former official of the Department of Homeland Security [DHS] should be reason enough to take the objections seriously on their substance, not just their politics.

Homeland security adviser Frances Townsend . . . said on national television that there is no notable difference between a British firm running the port operations in question and a UAE firm doing so. This statement is meant to suggest that only xenophobia [unreasonable fear of foreigners] can explain the actions of those who oppose the deal.

Ms. Townsend should know better.

1. The 9/11 commission was set up in 2002 to recount and respond to the terrorist attacks of 2001.

Caution Is Prudent

Leave aside what we clearly remember about the UAE's behavior in the not-too-distant past: that it recognized the Taliban government of Afghanistan, that it was the country of origin for two 9/11 hijackers and a nexus for much of the funding needed to organize that plot, and that the proliferation network of Pakistani scientist Abdul Qadeer Khan used UAE territory as a transshipment point for sensitive technologies.

Admittedly, these concerns are at least partially counterbalanced by the facts that the UAE has become a responsible player in port security on its own territory and that it has helped the United States substantially with intelligence cooperation and military bases in the war on terror.

But there is more to it.

In fact, existing policy draws a sharp distinction between close allies—allies such as Britain—and most of the world's other countries when it comes to vigilance against possible terrorism. Most relevant is the visa waiver program. Citizens from European states and a few other close allies need not have visas when coming to the United States; everyone else must.

This suggests that we recognize that our close democratic partners, whatever their own foibles, have better procedures for monitoring the proper behavior of their citizens than most other countries and a better means of fixing problems that become apparent.

The policy also underscores the point that, however reputable UAE officials are, however trustworthy the DPW management team may be, however nonviolent most UAE citizens undoubtedly are, there are nonetheless far more al Qaeda members living in the Middle East than in most other parts of the world.

Recognizing this does not make anyone racist. It is simply a fact.

The Risks of Outsourcing Aircraft Maintenance

When passengers board a commercial flight today [2008], there is a nearly 50% probability that the maintenance on their U.S. aircraft was performed not by FAA [Federal Aviation Administration]-certificated mechanics employed by an airline, but instead by workers at one of nearly 5,000 domestic and foreign contract repair stations.

As airlines have rushed to slash costs, aircraft maintenance outsourcing has increased significantly from 22.8% of maintenance expenditures for major U.S. airlines in 1995 to 45.9% in 2006.

Aircraft maintenance outsourcing is decimating what will be a hard-to-replace national asset: highly skilled aircraft and avionics technicians. In addition to safety and homeland security concerns, outsourcing is also tied to increased flight delays and cancellations. An examination of flight delay data shows that airlines with higher levels of maintenance outsourcing tend to have more delays blamed on the airline.

Coalition to Legislate Aircraft Maintenance Outsourcing Reform,
"Aircraft Maintenance Outsourcing Issues,"
March 2008. www.businesstravelcoalition.com.

That means there is a serious case for drawing a distinction between ownership of port operations by a British, a Korean or even a Singaporean firm and one run by a company in the UAE. (Whether Chinese firms should run U.S. ports is another matter, but a largely separate one.)

There is also a serious case for legislation proposed by Democratic Sens. Hillary Rodham Clinton of New York and

Robert Menendez of New Jersey to oppose foreign ownership of U.S. port operations, though this is a more drastic proposal and would require major changes to how things are done today.

The argument that DPW would not have responsibility for security operations at U.S. ports, which would remain in the hands of the Coast Guard and DHS, is partly right but incomplete.

Any firm managing cargo at such ports would necessarily know a great deal about the port, its shipping practices and its potential vulnerabilities. And even if DPW's current management is, as I suspect, entirely dependable in not wishing to misuse any such information, what assurance do we have that future employees hired into its management team will be as trustworthy?

Policy Change Could Make Outsourcing Port Security Possible

What to do?

If there is to be a useful compromise after 45 days, we need to begin by recognizing that it must have substantive elements. While much more needs to be done, I would suggest three broad areas for further investigation and brainstorming:

- The UAE government should not own DPW. Rather, the UAE needs to help us monitor the company in the future. Part of what makes democracies more trustworthy than autocracies (even benign ones, like the UAE) in these kinds of affairs is the system of checks and balances. With government ownership of the company at present, no such checks and balances can occur except on the U.S. end.

- We need to know more about intelligence-sharing between the two governments. While details must remain classified, the Bush administration must give unclassified reports to the public and hold more detailed private conversations with key members of Congress about what procedures can be instituted with the UAE so we can verify whatever checks it performs on its citizens who work for DPW. Perhaps much of this already happens, but as former Homeland Security Secretary Tom Ridge has pointed out, more transparency is needed.

• To show its good faith and make a contribution toward greater port security globally, the UAE should propose ways to help other countries improve port security. Creating a center on best practices within the Arab world would be one idea. Supporting research on even better practices, such as smart containers with sophisticated seals and global positioning systems allowing for full-time tracking of their whereabouts, would be another. Helping pay for improved procedures at ports in countries with less means to improve security themselves would be a third.

The blowup over DPW, however regrettable in one way, can still be turned into an opportunity for better policy if we approach it correctly. But that will require a greater shift in thinking on the subject than the Bush administration has demonstrated to date.

> *"[Dubai Ports World's] record globally indicates no more cause for concern than there would be with any other terminal operator—probably less."*

Outsourcing U.S. Port Operation Is Not a National Security Risk

James K. Glassman

James K. Glassman is a resident fellow at the American Enterprise Institute, whose research focuses on economic and financial issues. In the following viewpoint, which is his testimony before the Congressional Subcommittee on Domestic and International Monetary Policy, Glassman seeks to expose the presumptions that he believes wrongly underlie opposition to the outsourcing of port operation to United Arab Emirates (UAE) company Dubai Ports World (DPW). He cites UAE's recent positive interaction with the United States as evidence that DPW would run the ports as well as the British company that previously controlled them. And he notes that DPW has contracted with many other countries around the world to handle similar operations. Further, Glassman worries that the negative attitude many

James K. Glassman, "Threats to Security, Threats to Economy," *Testimony before the Subcommittee on Domestic and International Monetary Policy*, March 1, 2006. Copyright © 2005 American Enterprise Institute. All rights reserved. Reproduced by permission.

Americans had with regard to the DPW deal will damage U.S. relations with Arabic and Muslim countries.

As you read, consider the following questions:

1. What are some of the facts about United Arab Emirates given by the author to counter the statements of those who oppose the operation of American ports by Dubai Ports World?

2. What does the author fear will be the consequences if the United States develops "a reputation as a country that no longer welcomes some people's money"?

3. How, according to the author, should the United States address the threat of weapons of mass destruction being shipped into U.S. ports?

The feverish reaction of much of the media and many public officials to the imminent [2006] transfer of shipping-terminal operations at six U.S. ports raises disturbing questions about national-security priorities and about America's commitment to her staunchest allies and to the process of globalization.

At the heart of this reaction is a frightening specter: a dirty radioactive bomb or a full-fledged nuclear device shipped into a major city in one of the nine million trailer-sized containers that enter U.S. ports annually.

The fear of such an attack is a real concern, but the notion that a sale of assets to a Dubai company will increase the threat of such an attack is, emphatically, not.

Opposition Is Not Based on Facts

The recent uproar is puzzling in that it does not appear to fit the facts. For example, one member of the U.S. House [of Representatives] wrote President [George W.] Bush:

"In regards to selling American ports to the United Arab Emirates, not just NO—but HELL NO!"

Actually, no American ports will be sold to the United Arab Emirates [UAE]. The ports are owned by state and local authorities. A company called Dubai Ports World [DP World] based in the United Arab Emirates and currently doing business in such nations as Germany, Australia and the Dominican Republic, will, if the deal is fully consummated, take over terminal operations—the loading and unloading of trailer-sized containers—currently conducted by Peninsula & Oriental [P&O] Steam Navigation Co., based in London.

In another example, a U.S. Senator stated:

"Why in the world should we let this rogue government control ports in the United States?"

But the United Arab Emirates, formed in 1972 by seven small Persian Gulf states, is not a "rogue government." It is a nation of 2.6 million people with, according to the CIA Factbook, "an open economy with a high per capita income." The United States government has had close and friendly relations with the UAE, especially since the [terrorist] attacks of Sept. 11, 2001. Indeed, the UAE has been a model citizen in the region, recently entering into an important trade agreement.

Gen. Peter Pace, chairman of the Joint Chiefs of Staff, says that the U.S. has a "superb" military relationship with the UAE. "In everything that we have asked and worked with them on [including providing a base for U-2 spy planes and unmanned surveillance aircraft for fighting in Iraq and Afghanistan], they have proven to be very, very solid partners." It's doubtful that the U.S. would have sold 80 of the most sophisticated versions of the F-16 fighter jet to a "rogue government."

As a final example, another member of the U.S. House stated:

"Recently, the Bush Administration approved the takeover of six United States ports' security by Dubai Ports World. . . . The Bush Administration has been outsourcing jobs for five years, and now they want to outsource our national security."

In reality, primary responsibility for port security in the United States lies with the U.S. Coast Guard, the U.S. Customs, and Border Protection officials. In addition, most ports have their own law-enforcement authorities as well as local police. DP World also has responsibility for security, but its record globally indicates no more cause for concern than there would be with any other terminal operator—probably less.

As my colleague at the American Enterprise Institute, Veronique DeRugy, has written: "Foreign operation of American ports is nothing new. At least 30 percent of terminals at major U.S. ports are operated by foreign governments and businesses.... Ownership does not affect in any substantive way the dynamics of terrorist infiltration." Shipping security experts know that what is crucial is preventing nuclear material from being placed on vessels in foreign ports in the first place....

United Arab Emirates Is an Ally in the Middle East

Prior to the attacks of 9/11, the UAE was one of only three governments (the others were Pakistan and Saudi Arabia) that recognized the Taliban in Afghanistan. After the attacks, all three countries immediately cut their ties. The UAE was home to two of the 9/11 hijackers, and the FBI has said that the UAE banking system was used to transfer funds to the hijackers. In addition, according to *The Economist*, "A.Q. [Abdul Qadeer] Khan's Pakistani nuclear-smuggling network ... was hidden behind a Dubai front."

However, since the war on terror began, the UAE has been a staunch U.S. ally, providing "significant assistance both in passing along terrorism tips and in helping to apprehend suspects" [as reported by the *Wall Street Journal*].

The UAE has provided services for 700 U.S. Navy ships a year at its ports, including the DP World-operated terminal of

Jebel Ali. In fact, the UAE hosts more U.S. Navy visits than any port outside the United States, and Dubai is a popular port for sailors on leave. As former secretary of the Navy Will Ball recently wrote on TCSDaily.com: "In a region of the world not previously known for 'liberty ports' that compete with their Mediterranean and Western Pacific counterparts, the new Dubai is fine, fine indeed, according to the sailors of today. Harbormasters, citizens and yes, even port security officials there afford an especially warm welcome to American warships—aircraft carriers in particular."

DP World is also the primary support contractor for U.S. Air Force assets at Al Dhafra Air Base, where refueling and reconnaissance flights originate for southwest Asia.

The Appearance of Prejudice

By any objective analysis, the United Arab Emirates has embraced the security and economic prescriptions of the United States. "Dubai," says a news article in the Feb. 26 [2006] edition of the *Financial Times*, "has gone out of its way to project an image as a pragmatic, pro-Western and free-market exception in a region often bristling with hostility to America."

Al-Maktoum, Dubai's ruler, not only has developed Jebel Ali into a huge free port, one of the largest in the world. He has also created one of the world's largest airlines, Emirates, and launched what *Business Week* calls "a new financial center that is attracting the cream of the world's banks."

At the very least, the reaction to the purchase of P&O has similarly pro-Western business leaders in the Arab and Muslim world scratching their heads in bewilderment and wondering whether racial prejudice, misinformation or paranoia is behind the hysteria.

One could argue that the UAE is at least as strong an ally of the U.S. in the war on terror as France. Yet a French company, Suez, owns plants in 17 states that provide seven million Americans with drinking water daily. An article in *Lloyd's List*, the shipping newspaper, noted: "Venezuela's Hugo Chavez, whose opinions about President George W. Bush and Secretary of State Condoleezza Rice would make a lesser man and woman blush, controls Citgo, and its terminal and refinery in Philadelphia." While it's true that two 9/11 terrorists came from the UAE, it's also true that the man who attempted to set off a shoe bomb on a transatlantic flight was a British citizen, and several U.S. citizens have been arrested as terrorist suspects as well.

Meanwhile, DP World's purchase of terminal operations in Germany and Australia—countries that have concerns about terrorism similar to those in the United States (more Australian civilians have been killed by terrorists since 9/11 than American civilians)—produced no notice at all. "I can't really see the security question coming up as DP World is a well established, respectable company," said Patrick Verhoeven, secretary general of the European Sea Ports Organization.

Outcry Threatens Future Investments

The overreaction of many public officials in the United States to the terminal transactions, coupled with Congress's recent thwarting of the purchase of Unocal by a Chinese company, cannot help but deter other investments, especially by developing nations, in this country. "Xenophobia," as *The Economist* put it, "seems to be creeping into American politics."

The arithmetic of foreign investment is not complicated. The current account deficit has been rising for the past decade and now is 6 percent of GDP [gross domestic product], indicating a wide gap between what we buy, in goods and services, from foreigners and what we sell to them. This deficit has not harmed the U.S. economy for a simple reason: the United States remains one of the best places in the world to invest. So dollars that flow abroad from our purchase of imports are recycled back to us as capital investments.

Initiatives Can Ensure Secure Outsourcing

Applying protectionist policies to homeland security would stifle innovation and increase costs—working against the DHS [Department of Homeland Security] goal of getting the best security for the dollars invested. Where the contract is fulfilled—whether in Boston, Britain, or Bermuda—does not necessarily add to or detract from the end goal of protecting America. . . . It is imperative that DHS award contracts to companies that both meet those security standards *and* possess the expertise to complete the projects. In general, DHS should insist that contract work is conducted in countries that have a cooperative relationship with the United States across a broad spectrum of security initiatives, including:

- Harmonization of security requirements and acquisition processes;

- Security of supply;

- Export procedures;

- Security of information;

- Ownership and corporate governance;

- Research and development;

- Flow of technical information; and

- Security trade.

James Jay Carafano et al., "Protectionism Compromises America's Homeland Security," Backgrounder, no. 1777, July 9, 2004. www.heritage.org.

At the end of 2004 . . . , foreigners owned about $12 trillion in U.S. assets: $6 trillion in stocks and bonds, $3 trillion in debt to banks and other lenders and $3 trillion in hard assets, like factories. These capital flows employ Americans, raise their paychecks and keep interest rates down.

In recent years, important capital flows are coming from emerging markets, including Asia and the Middle East. These flows are expected to continue—and not just because of oil. As Jeremy Siegel writes, demographic imbalances mean that older people in the U.S. and other developed nations will have to live off the sale of assets to younger people in developing nations.

At any rate, the continuing free flow of capital into the United States is crucial. [The *Financial Times* reports that] Dubai has been among the "most prominent recent buyers into the U.S. economy," with, for example, Dubai International Capital buying a 2 percent stake in Daimler Chrysler . . . [in 2005].

Now, however, the United States risks developing a reputation as a country that no longer welcomes some people's money. If that happens, other nations—Japan, Britain, Germany, Australia—will attract capital that would have gone to the U.S. The virtuous circle of global trade and investment risks being broken, with disastrous consequences.

That is the real danger here. We shouldn't flatter ourselves. We aren't the center of the world. Look at shipping terminals. The action is not in New York or Los Angeles. It's in Singapore, Hong Kong, and new ports in Shanghai, South Korea and India.

Addressing the Root of Security Issues

This episode has been a sad one in many ways, but it could help revive interest among policy makers in getting serious about reducing the threat of seaborne weapons of mass destruction. That threat must be attacked at the source. "Our first priority," writes Veronique DeRugy of AEI, "should be to stop terrorists from acquiring fissile material to build a bomb." But just $250 million is spent in these efforts. Our second priority should be to stop such material from getting on ships in foreign ports. DHS's [Department of Homeland Security's] Container Security Initiative, in which the Dubai participates, inspects cargo for WMD [weapons of mass destruction] before it is shipped. But only $139 million was spent on this program ... [in 2005]. The third priority is security in U.S. ports themselves, where $360 million is spent on in-port detection devices. Far more resources—human, technological and financial—must be devoted to preventing WMD from ever being loaded on a ship.

Would withdrawing the P&O leases from DP World help national security? That's a dubious proposition. It would certainly jeopardize Dubai's role as a loyal American ally—if that role has not been jeopardized already.

> *"The new e-passports could be compro-*
> *mised and sold on the black market for*
> *use by terrorists or other foreign en-*
> *emies."*

Outsourcing Passport Production Is a Risk to National Security

Bill Gertz

Bill Gertz is a reporter for The Washington Times *newspaper, covering defense and national security topics, and most recently the author of the book* Enemies: How America's Foes Steal Our Vital Secrets and How We Let It Happen. *In the following viewpoint, he investigates the possible threats to national security that could result from the outsourcing of U.S. passport produc-tion. Gertz contends that allowing the passports to be produced in countries such as Thailand that have questionable records when it comes to combating terrorism, and then using unsecured transportation methods to send the passports to U.S. offices could result in shipments of blank passports landing in the hands of terrorists or others wishing to do harm to the country. The au-thor further reveals that the motive for outsourcing appears to be*

*increased profits for a government agency charged with creating
passports at cost for American citizens.*

As you read, consider the following questions:

1. According to Gertz, how are the new e-passports more
   secure than previous passports?
2. What are the two main flaws in passport production
   addressed by Gertz?
3. According to Michelle Van Cleave, how would the compromising of passport integrity impact national security
   apart from concerns about terrorists using them to impose direct harm on the country?

The United States has outsourced the manufacturing of its
electronic passports to overseas companies—including
one in Thailand that was victimized by Chinese espionage—
raising concerns that cost savings are being put ahead of national security, an investigation by *The Washington Times* has
found.

The Government Printing Office's [GPO] decision to export the work has proved lucrative, allowing the agency to
book more than $100 million in recent profits by charging the
State Department more money for blank passports than it actually costs to make them, according to interviews with federal
officials and documents obtained by *The Times*.

The profits have raised questions both inside the agency
and in Congress because the law that created GPO as the federal government's official printer explicitly requires the agency
to break even by charging only enough to recover its costs.

Lawmakers Voice Concerns

Lawmakers said they were alarmed by *The Times'* findings and
plan to investigate why U.S. companies weren't used to produce the state-of-the-art passports, one of the crown jewels of
American border security.

"I am not only troubled that there may be serious security concerns with the new passport production system, but also that GPO officials may have been profiting from producing them," said Rep. John D. Dingell, the Michigan Democrat who chairs the House Energy and Commerce Committee.

Officials at GPO, the Homeland Security Department and the State Department played down such concerns, saying they are confident that regular audits and other protections already in place will keep terrorists and foreign spies from stealing or copying the sensitive components to make fake passports.

"Aside from the fact that we have fully vetted and qualified vendors, we also note that the materials are moved via a secure transportation means, including armored vehicles," GPO spokesman Gary Somerset said.

But GPO Inspector General J. Anthony Ogden, the agency's internal watchdog, doesn't share that confidence. He warned in an internal . . . report that there are "significant deficiencies with the manufacturing of blank passports, security of components, and the internal controls for the process."

The inspector general's report said GPO claimed it could not improve its security because of "monetary constraints." But the inspector general recently told congressional investigators he was unaware that the agency had booked tens of millions of dollars in profits through passport sales that could have been used to improve security, congressional aides told *The Times.*

Security Concerns in Passport Production

GPO is an agency little-known to most Americans, created by Congress almost two centuries ago as a virtual monopoly to print nearly all of the government's documents, from federal agency reports to the president's massive budget books that outline every penny of annual federal spending. Since 1926, it also has been charged with the job of printing the passports used by Americans to enter and leave the country.

When the government moved a few years ago to a new electronic passport designed to foil counterfeiting, GPO led the work of contracting with vendors to install the technology.

Each new e-passport contains a small computer chip inside the back cover that contains the passport number along with the photo and other personal data of the holder. The data is secured and is transmitted through a tiny wire antenna when it is scanned electronically at border entry points and compared to the actual traveler carrying it.

According to interviews and documents, GPO managers rejected limiting the contracts to U.S.-made computer chip makers and instead sought suppliers from several countries, including Israel, Germany and the Netherlands.

Mr. Somerset, the GPO spokesman, said foreign suppliers were picked because "no domestic company produced those parts" when the e-passport production began a few years ago.

After the computer chips are inserted into the back cover of the passports in Europe, the blank covers are shipped to a factory in Ayutthaya, Thailand, north of Bangkok, to be fitted with a wire Radio Frequency Identification, or RFID, antenna. The blank passports eventually are transported to Washington for final binding, according to the documents and interviews.

The stop in Thailand raises its own security concerns. The Southeast Asian country has battled social instability and terror threats. Anti-government groups backed by Islamists, including al Qaeda, have carried out attacks in southern Thailand and the Thai military took over in a coup in September 2006.

The Netherlands-based company that assembles the U.S. e-passport covers in Thailand, Smartrac Technology Ltd., warned in its latest annual report that, in a worst-case scenario, social unrest in Thailand could lead to a halt in production.

Smartrac divulged in an October 2007 court filing in The Hague [a city in the Netherlands] that China had stolen its patented technology for e-passport chips, raising additional questions about the security of America's e-passports.

The Threat of Losing Blank Passports

A 2005 document obtained by *The Times* states that GPO was using unsecure FedEx courier services to send blank passports to State Department offices until security concerns were raised and forced GPO to use an armored car company. Even then, the agency proposed using a foreign armored car vendor before State Department diplomatic security officials objected.

Concerns that GPO has been lax in addressing security threats contrast with the very real danger that the new e-passports could be compromised and sold on the black market for use by terrorists or other foreign enemies, experts said.

"The most dangerous passports, and the ones we have to be most concerned about, are stolen blank passports," said Ronald K. Noble, secretary general of Interpol, the Lyon, France-based international police organization. "They are the most dangerous because they are the most difficult to detect."

Mr. Noble said no counterfeit e-passports have been found yet, but the potential is "a great weakness and an area that world governments are not paying enough attention to."

Lukas Grunwald, a computer security expert, said U.S. e-passports, like their European counterparts, are vulnerable to copying and that their shipment overseas during production increases the risks. "You need a blank passport and a chip and once you do that, you can do anything, you can make a fake passport, you can change the data," he said.

Separately, Rep. Robert A. Brady, chairman of the Joint Committee on Printing, has expressed "serious reservations" about GPO's plan to use contract security guards to protect GPO facilities. In a Dec. 12 [2007] letter, Mr. Brady, a Penn-

National Security Threats Increase as Outsourcing Increases

American national security is increasingly dependent on the superiority of the country's technological innovations and the intellectual knowledge of its citizens. Necessary advances result from a combination of research, government-funded academic work, and industry experience. Unfortunately, during the past decade communication, semiconductor manufacturing, electronic device design, software, entertainment, pharmaceutical, and other key technological capabilities and intellectual activities have been shipped overseas....

As offshore companies grow in capability, the United States is at great risk of losing its technological dominance to countries such as India, China, and some of the European countries. This may result in the closing of the gap between high-speed communications research and development for military applications and the development of products for commercial use, giving regional competitors, criminal networks, and terrorists an improved position in information warfare. At the very least, American technical power, and by extension its military power—especially aspects based on international communications networks—may be severely at risk.

Batoul Modarress and Al Ansari, "The Economic, Technological, and National Security Risks of Offshore Outsourcing," The Journal of Global Business Issues, Summer 2007.

sylvania Democrat, stated that GPO's plan for conducting a security review of the printing office was ignored and he ordered GPO to undertake an outside review.

Profits for a Nonprofit Agency

GPO's accounting adds another layer of concern.

The State Department is now charging Americans $100 or more for new e-passports produced by the GPO, depending on how quickly they are needed. That's up from a cost of around just $60 in 1998.

Internal agency documents obtained by *The Times* show each blank passport costs GPO an average of just $7.97 to manufacture and that GPO then charges the State Department about $14.80 for each, a margin of more than 85 percent, the documents show.

The accounting allowed GPO to make gross profits of more than $90 million from Oct. 1, 2006, through Sept. 30, 2007, on the production of e-passports. The four subsequent months produced an additional $54 million in gross profits.

The agency set aside more than $40 million of those profits to help build a secure backup passport production facility in the South, still leaving a net profit of about $100 million. . . . GPO was initially authorized by Congress to make extra profits in order to fund a $41 million backup production facility at a rate of $1.84 per passport. The large surplus, however, went far beyond the targeted funding.

The large profits raised concerns within GPO because the law traditionally has mandated that the agency only charge enough to recoup its actual costs.

According to internal documents and interviews, GPO's financial officers and even its outside accounting firm began to inquire about the legality of the e-passport profits.

To cut off the debate, GPO's outgoing legal counsel signed a one-paragraph memo last fall [2007] declaring the agency was in compliance with the law prohibiting profits, but offering no legal authority to back up the conclusion. The large profits accelerated, according to the officials, after the opinion issued Oct. 12, 2007, by then-GPO General Counsel Gregory

A. Brower. Mr. Brower, currently U.S. Attorney in Nevada, could not be reached and his spokeswoman had no immediate comment.

Fred Antoun, a lawyer who specializes in GPO funding issues, said the agency was set up by Congress to operate basically on a break-even financial basis.

"The whole concept of GPO is eat what you kill," Mr. Antoun said. "For the average taxpayer, for them to make large profits is kind of reprehensible."

Likewise, a 1990 report by Congress' General Accounting Office stated that "by law, GPO must charge actual costs to customers," meaning it can't mark up products for a profit.

A Result of Increased Demand

Like the security concerns, GPO officials brush aside questions about the profits. Agency officials declined a request from *The Times* to provide an exact accounting of its e-passport costs and revenues, saying only it would not be accurate to claim it has earned the large profits indicated by the documents showing the difference between the manufacturing costs and the State Department fees.

Questioned about its own annual report showing a $90 million-plus profit on e-passports in fiscal year 2007 alone, the GPO spokesman Mr. Somerset would only say that he thinks the agency is in legal compliance and that "GPO is not overcharging the State Department."

Mr. Somerset said 66 different budget line items are used to price new passports and "we periodically review our pricing structure with the State Department."

Public Printer Robert Tapella, the GPO's top executive, faced similar questions during a House subcommittee hearing on March 6 [2008]. Mr. Tapella told lawmakers that increased demand for passports—especially from Americans who now need them to cross into Mexico and Canada—produced "accelerated revenue recognition," and "not necessarily excess profits."

GPO plans to produce 28 million blank passports ... [in 2008] up from about 9 million five years ago.

Periodical Bibliography

The following articles have been selected to supplement the diverse views presented in this chapter.

Brian Bennett   "Outsourcing the War," *Time*, March 26, 2007.

Christian   "Outsourcing U.S. Security," March 10, 2008.
Science Monitor

Adam Ely   "Shore Up Data Sent Offshore," *Information Week*, June 2, 2008.

Foreign Policy   "Spies for Hire," March-April 2008.

Harry Hurt III   "The Business of Intelligence Gathering," *New York Times*, June 15, 2008.

Sushill Kumar   "How to Protect Data in Outsourcing Deals," *Managing Intellectual Property*, March 2007.

Marvin Leibstone   "Military Outsourcing—Healing the Cuts," *Military Technology*, 2007.

Shawn Macomber   "You're Not in the Army Now," *American Spectator*, November 2004.

Clay Risen   "War-Mart," *New Republic*, April 3, 2006.

Rai Saritha   "Security Breaches Worry Outsourcing Industry," *New York Times*, October 5, 2006.

Jeremy Scahill   "Blackwater's Private Spies," *Nation*, June 23, 2008.

Geri Smith and   "The Offshoring of Airplane Care," *Business*
Justin Bachman   *Week Online*, April 10, 2008. www.businessweek.com.

Mathias Thurman   "Offshore Security Is out of Sight, Not out of Mind," *Computerworld*, May 8, 2006.

OPPOSING
VIEWPOINTS®
SERIES

CHAPTER 3

How Should the Government Regulate Outsourcing?

Chapter Preface

When questioned about the need for outsourcing jobs to other nations, many American companies respond that they have no choice but to fill positions with lower cost, aptly skilled foreigners to stay competitive in the new era of globalization. But some economists maintain that the best interests of a corporation do not always correspond to the best interests of America. They fear that offshoring thousands of jobs to low-paid workers drives down the wages of American employees with similar skills and robs them of the achievement of middle class status. According to a 2004 Zogby International poll, three in five Americans believe that the solution to this problem is to have the U.S. government "tax or legislate against companies who engage in outsourcing."

Currently few federal laws limit outsourcing. The government has created regulations that restrict financial institutions and health organizations from passing personal information overseas. More recently, President George W. Bush signed the Thomas-Voinovich Amendment as part of the Omnibus Appropriations Bill in 2004. The Thomas-Voinovich Amendment states that some federal contract work must be performed within the United States unless it was previously performed outside the country.

A similar bill was passed in 1933 to compel government agencies to purchase goods from domestic suppliers unless the comparative cost was burdensome. Government offices, however, have easily bypassed the Buy American Act, as the 1933 bill is titled, claiming that certain domestic goods do not satisfy the demanded quantity or quality or that purchasing domestically is not within the vaguely defined public interest. In the following chapter, U.S. Senator Russ Feingold, a Democrat from Wisconsin, argues that the Buy American Act needs to be strengthened to eliminate these loopholes and compel the government to shop for domestic goods before considering foreign purchases.

Feingold has his detractors, though. Many economists who favor a globalized economy contend that free trade should determine business practices, not government mandates. They stipulate that businesses look to foreign lands not only for cheaper labor but also for talents and skills that U.S. workers might not be offering. As one side of a 2007 *Business Week* debate argues, "If one country is better at making wine and the other bread, both countries come out ahead if they specialize their skills and then trade with each other. Outsourcing is nothing more than trading services, instead of goods, across international borders." To try to impose restrictions on free trade, advocates say, could be damaging to the U.S. economy and may even violate the trade agreements America has established with global markets.

Supporters and opponents of the government regulation of outsourcing have their say in the following chapter. While some, like Senator Feingold, worry that Congress is not doing enough to stop the flight of jobs overseas, others believe that America cannot maintain financial security in a globalized economy if it tries to remain protectionist.

> *"Rather than filling skills shortages as originally conceived, the H-1B program in practice gives employers a temptation, cheaper labor, they simply can't resist."*

Guest Worker Visa Programs Should Be Limited

Ron Hira

Ron Hira claims in the following viewpoint that H-1B guest worker visas are harming American workers in the technology and service fields. Hira asserts that these visas are being handed out in the thousands to foreigners because companies in the United States benefit from the glut of overseas technicians who will work for relatively low wages. American workers lose out on these jobs and also lose their competitive edge in global markets, Hira contends, when the guest workers take the skills they learned at American companies back to their homelands. Hira maintains that the government needs to limit such outsourcing and invest at home. Ron Hira is a professor of public policy at Rochester Institute of Technology and the author of Outsourcing America: What's Behind Our National Crisis and How We Can Reclaim American Jobs.

Ron Hira, "How 'Guestworkers' Promote Outsourcing," *American Prospect*, August 6, 2007. Reproduced with permission from The American Prospect, 11 Beacon Street, Suite 1120, Boston, MA 02108.

As you read, consider the following questions:

1. Why does Hira complain about the visa requirement by which guest workers should be paid the prevailing wage in their field?
2. What problem does Hira have with the labor certification process for foreign guest workers?
3. What problems with the American technological labor market are exacerbated by the guest worker visa program, in the author's opinion?

The H-1B "guestworker" program allows firms to bring foreign workers on a temporary basis in so-called specialty occupations, generally professional positions that require a bachelor's degree or higher. It is extensively used by the technology industry to bring in information technology workers. The program has been the focal point of the high-skilled side of the immigration policy debate, and was a significant part of the negotiations in ... [a failed 2007] comprehensive immigration bill considered by the Senate.

But there is a huge amount of mythology about what this program actually does.

A lobbying coalition of the technology industry and universities is seeking a massive increase in the annual quota of H-1B visas. The group has repeatedly pointed to the fact that the annual H-1B quota of 65,000 visas was filled in a single day as proof that the quota is too small. They pulled out all the stops, enlisting [former CEO of Microsoft] Bill Gates in the lobbying effort. In testimony before the Senate he called for an unlimited number of H-1B visas, portraying the typical visa recipient as a uniquely talented engineer earning more than $100,000 per year.

The carefully orchestrated public relations blitz included support from editorial boards of major newspapers and well placed news articles. Most complained that America was shooting itself in the foot by not importing workers for jobs that Americans are *incapable* of performing. And if persuasion wasn't enough, the technology industry used the not-so-subtle threat that it will simply shift the work offshore if it can't import workers.

Training Foreigners to Compete with Americans

A number of presidential candidates have taken the bait by publicly supporting an H-1B increase. The deep pocketed technology industry has made it clear to them it wants something in return for being an ATM to the candidates.

But in reality, the H-1B program has been thoroughly corrupted. Rather than providing firms with workers who posses unique skills, the program is dominated by low wage workers with ordinary rank-and-file skills. And rather than preventing work from going overseas, the program is speeding it up.

Offshore outsourcing firms rely on the H-1B and related L-1 programs for three principal reasons. First, it facilitates their knowledge-transfer operations, where they rotate in foreign workers to learn U.S. workers' jobs. In fact, U.S. workers are often "transferring knowledge" under duress.

Second, the H-1B and L-1 programs provide them an inexpensive, on-site presence that enables them to coordinate offshore functions. Many functions that are done remotely still require a significant amount of physical presence at the customer site. For example, according to its own financial reporting, Infosys's on-site workers, almost all of whom are foreign guestworkers, directly accounted for 49.2 percent of its revenue in its most recent quarter.

Third, the H-1B and L-1 programs allow the U.S. operations to serve as a training ground for foreign workers who then rotate back to their home country to do the work more effectively than they could have without such training in the United States. A recent *Business Week* story described Wipro's use of the H-1B program this way: "Wipro has more than

4,000 employees in the United States, and roughly 2,500 are on H-1B visas. About 1,000 new temporary workers come to the country each year, while 1,000 rotate back to India, with improved skills to serve clients."

Overlooking Qualified Americans

The abuse of the program is the result of three loopholes.

The first loophole strikes right at the heart of the rationale for the program—the supposed shortage of workers with specialized skills, particularly in science and engineering; the H-1B program allows firms to hire foreign guest-workers to fill those gaps. But, because of this loophole, companies do not have to demonstrate a shortage exists for U.S. workers and can even force a U.S. worker to train his or her foreign replacement. The U.S. Department of Labor's 2006 Strategic Plan puts it bluntly, "H-1B workers may be hired even when a qualified U.S. worker wants the job, and a U.S. worker can be displaced from the job in favor of the foreign worker."

In spite of this unequivocal statement, there is widespread and mistaken public belief that firms must demonstrate a shortage before hiring an H-1B. For example, news stories [in 2006] in the *New York Times, Los Angeles Times, San Diego Union-Tribune,* and *Wall Street Journal* have all erroneously claimed the program requires firms to first look for American workers. And the *New York Daily News* even recently made the false claim in editorial support for H-1B expansion. Many politicians also hold this misconception, making similarly false claims in their correspondence in response to constituent letters on the matter.

Importing Low Wage Workers

The second loophole enables firms to use the program for cheap labor. The H-1B program's primary safeguard for U.S. as well as H-1B workers is the requirement that an H-1B worker be paid the *prevailing wage.* In theory the prevailing wage should be at least the market wage—the wage paid to an American worker with the same skills—but in practice the regulation is chock full of loopholes allowing employers to pay below market wages. How do we know this? Employers say so. The Government Accountability Office [GAO] conducted interviews of H-1B employers and reported that, "Some employers said that they hired H-1B workers in part because these workers would often accept lower salaries than similarly qualified U.S. workers; however, these employers said they never paid H-1B workers less than the required [prevailing] wage."

And examples of approved H-1B applications show how big the cost savings can be. In 2006, the U.S. Department of Labor (DOL) rubber-stamped applications by HCL America, a major offshore outsourcing firm, to import 75 computer software engineers at annual salary of $24,710. That's a 70 percent discount on the median wage rate for those occupations and a far cry from the $100,000 claimed by Microsoft's Bill Gates. In fact low wages for H-1Bs is the norm. The median wage for new H-1Bs computing professionals is even lower than the salary an *entry-level* bachelor's degree graduate would command. So, half of the 52,352 H-1B computing professionals admitted in FY [fiscal year] 2005 earned less than entry-level wages. And even at the 75th percentile, now H-1B computing professionals earned just $60,000. A recent study by John Miano [founder of the Programming Guild, an organization concerned about outsourcing] found that 56 percent of the H-1B applications for computing jobs were for the lowest skill level, "Level 1." The DOL defines such jobs as "internships" or "workers in training."

No Oversight of the Guestworker Process

A third problem, deficient oversight, permeates nearly all aspects of the H-1B program. This leads to a program with pages of regulations that are essentially ineffective and toothless. The DOL's own Office of Inspector General has described the labor certification process, the primary means of safeguarding the labor market, as simply a "rubber stamp" of the employer's application. The process is completely automated, with no person reviewing applications, and the employer is not required to submit any supporting documentation. Based on its examination of the process, the GAO concluded that, ". . . as the [H-1B] program currently operates, the goals of preventing abuse of the program and providing efficient services to employers and workers are not being achieved. Limited by the law, Labor's review of the [labor certification process] is perfunctory and adds little assurance that labor conditions employers attest to actually exist."

And it is no better after an H-1B is issued. Employers are never scrutinized except in the rare case that an investigation is triggered by an H-1B worker whistleblower, something that is exceptionally rare since H-1B employees have especially strong disincentives to blow the whistle on their employer. Because the employer holds the visa, an H-1B worker who gets terminated is out of status (they would have to leave the country) in the eyes of the USCIS [Bureau of U.S. Citizenship and Immigration Services]. With cases against employers often taking five or more years to adjudicate, it is no wonder that few violations are ever brought to the attention of the DOL.

Americans Are Losing Out on Jobs

Any one of these flaws would cause a program to fail to meet its goals. Couple them together and the result is a disaster, a program that directly contradicts its goals. Rather than filling skills shortages as originally conceived, the H-1B program in practice gives employers a temptation, cheaper labor, they simply can't resist. The *raison d'etre* [purpose] of modern corporations is maximizing profits, not maximizing their U.S. workforce or increasing the economic welfare of the United States. If companies can lower costs by hiring cheaper foreign

Cheap Workers Drive Down Wages

Simply having a large influx of workers into the industry floods the labor market and drives down wages. Study after study shows that H-1B workers are paid lower wages than their American counterparts, driving down the prevailing wage: A UCLA [University of California, Los Angeles] study found that H-1B engineers were paid 33 percent less than comparable U.S. citizens. A Cornell University study found that H-1B programmers and engineers were underpaid by 20 to 30 percent. . . . A National Research Council report found that "H-1B workers requiring lower levels of high tech skill received lower wages, less senior job titles, smaller signing bonuses, and smaller pay and compensation increases than would be typical for the work they did." It also found that H-1Bs have an adverse impact on overall wage levels. The Independent Computer Consultants Association reports that the use of cheaper foreign labor has forced down the hourly rates of U.S. consultants by as much as 10 to 40 percent.

Federation for American Immigration Reform,
"H-1B Visas: Harming American Workers,"
April 2008. www.fairus.org.

guestworkers, they will. If they can hire vendors who hire cheaper foreign guestworkers, they will. And who can blame them? If they don't take advantage of blatant loopholes, their competitors surely will. Cheap labor explains why the H-1B program is oversubscribed and it also explains why the technology industry has fought to expand government intervention to keep wages low. A sizable share of the U.S. high-tech workforce understands this logic, and justifiably views the

H-1B program as a threat and a scam. That's the real danger to U.S. competitiveness. Young people considering a technology career see that industry prefers cheaper foreign guestworkers and that the government uses immigration policy to work against technology professionals.

Another canard from the industry lobbyists is that the H-1B program prevents outsourcing. Instead, the facts clearly show it is speeding up the outsourcing of jobs. Seven of the top ten H-1B employers are offshore outsourcing firms—firms that hire almost no Americans. Those seven firms gobbled up nearly 20,000 visas in 2006 alone. And each of those 20,000 positions is used to lever four to five more workers overseas. Many American politicians act oblivious to what is obvious to India's Commerce Minister, Kamal Nath, who recently dubbed the H-1B the "outsourcing visa." The Indian government views the H-1B as a trade issue, not an immigration one. As such they view any restriction on the movement of people in the form of wage requirements or caps as a non-tariff barrier to trade. Their comparative advantage is low cost labor and Corporate America is lobbying hard to help push through this form of "free trade."

Exacerbating Other Problems in the U.S. Labor Market

The technology industry claims the United States doesn't produce enough technologists. This claim is specious at best. Wages for information technology workers have been relatively flat while the career risks for the profession have skyrocketed. The industry's track record of attracting female and underrepresented minorities to technical professions has been woeful. By giving the industry a steady diet of cheap labor, there is no reason for companies to expand the domestic talent pool they draw from and invest in American workers to fill these jobs. And it also gives the companies ample opportunities to replace older workers with younger ones, fueling age discrimination. If more than half of the H-1B jobs being filled are for "internships" and "workers in training" then it shouldn't be difficult to pull more Americans into the high-skill ranks.

Fortunately, some politicians are paying attention. The Senate immigration bill included more than just an increase in the number of H-1Bs, it also contained some, though not nearly enough, substantive reforms to the program. Senators Dick Durbin and Charles Grassley, who introduced separate legislation to clean up the H-1B and its lesser known sister program, the L-1, played a key role in ensuring that reforms were included in the comprehensive bill. While the H-1B program's regulations are riddled with loopholes, the L-1 program has almost no regulations—no wage requirements and no cap.

Invest at Home

Guestworker programs like the H-1B and L-1 shouldn't be confused with permanent immigration, something the technology lobbyists have used in their public relations efforts. They falsely claim that increasing high-skilled permanent immigration is contingent on an increase in H-1Bs. If we want to increase the number of high-skilled Americans through higher levels of immigration, then let's make them permanent residents, not guestworkers.

The technology industry has long complained about a systemic shortage of workers, but the only solution it offers is for the government to intervene in the labor market by ratcheting up guestworker programs. Technology executives like Intel's Craig Barrett publicly lambaste our K–12 education system as a complete failure leading to an inadequate pipeline of American workers capable of doing technology. At the same time, his company aggressively plays one state government against another as it pursues property tax breaks when locating a facility. A more sensible set of solutions would be twofold. First, significantly increase investments in U.S. students and under-employed workers so they can fill these job openings. Second, let the market work. If technology workers are as scarce as companies claim, then wages would be bid up and talented workers would choose engineering instead of more lucrative and safe fields in finance, medicine or law.

A country with an effective labor-market policy would have no H-1B program at all.

| "The simple fact is that highly skilled foreign-born workers make enormous contributions to our economy."

Guest Worker Visa Programs Should Be Expanded

William H. Gates

The following viewpoint is written testimony that Microsoft chairman William H. Gates delivered to the U.S. House of Representatives Committee on Science and Technology. In the viewpoint, Gates urges the committee to take action and reform the guest worker visa program in the United States. According to Gates, America is not producing enough science, technology, engineering, and math graduates, leaving shortages in high-tech corporations that do business in the country. Gates insists that foreign-born technicians can fill these positions if only Congress and the President would relax restrictions on H-1B guest worker visas and raise the quotas of foreigners who can work in the United States. If the government fails to act, Gates says, these industries may find it increasingly difficult to compete in a global market.

William H. Gates, Testimony Before the Committee on Science and Technology United States House of Representatives, March 12, 2008.

As you read, consider the following questions:

1. For what two urgent reasons should Americans be deeply concerned that the nation's science and technology advantages are slipping away, in Gates's view?

2. According to Gates, by what percentage has the number of U.S. undergraduate engineering degrees fallen between 1985 and 2005?

3. As Gates explains, on what significant day did the supply of H-1B visas for fiscal year 2008 run out?

During the last 50 years, the world has witnessed truly revolutionary advances in science and technology. We as a nation can take pride in knowing that American scientists, researchers, and entrepreneurs have been at the forefront of many of these advances. Our unmatched ability to turn new ideas in science and technology into thriving businesses has been the engine of growth and job creation that has made our economy among the most dynamic and competitive in the world. . . .

A Lack of Educated Technicians

I am optimistic about the potential for technology to help us find new ways to improve people's lives and tackle important challenges. I am less optimistic, however, that the United States will continue to remain a global leader in technology innovation. While America's innovation heritage is unparalleled, the evidence is mounting that we are failing to make the investments in our young people, our workers, our scientific research infrastructure, and our economy that will enable us to retain our global innovation leadership.

In particular, I believe that there are two urgent reasons why we should all be deeply concerned that our advantages in science and technology innovation are in danger of slipping away.

First, we face a critical shortfall of skilled scientists and engineers who can develop new breakthrough technologies. Second, the public and private sectors are no longer investing in basic research and development (R&D) at the levels needed to drive long-term innovation.

If the United States truly wants to secure its global leadership in technology innovation, we must, as a nation, commit to a strategy for innovation excellence—a set of initiatives and policies that will provide the foundation for American competitive strength in the years ahead. . . .

Like many others, I have deep misgivings about the state of education in the United States. Too many of our students fail to graduate from high school with the basic skills they will need to succeed in the 21st century economy, much less prepared for the rigors of college and career. Although our top universities continue to rank among the best in the world, too few American students are pursuing degrees in science and technology. Compounding this problem is our failure to provide sufficient training for those already in the workforce. . . .

Unfortunately, we are not graduating enough students with degrees in the STEM [science, technology, engineering, and math] disciplines to meet the growing demand from U.S. companies for workers in these areas. Without people who have the skills necessary to drive the next wave of technology innovation, it will be impossible for the United States to retain its global innovation leadership.

Consider these facts. The U.S. Department of Labor has projected that by 2014, there will be more than two million job openings in the United States in STEM fields. Yet the number of American students graduating with degrees in these fields is actually *declining*. Indeed, the number of undergraduate engineering degrees awarded in the United States fell by about 15 percent between 1985 and 2005. This decline is particularly alarming when we look at educational trends in other countries, many of which award a higher percentage of college degrees in engineering than does the United States. . . .

Guest Worker Quotas Are Too Small

If we are going to address the shortage of scientists and engineers . . . [we must reconsider] our immigration rules for highly skilled workers. Today, knowledge and expertise are the essential raw materials that companies and countries need in order to be competitive. We live in an economy that depends on the ability of innovative companies to attract and retain the very best talent, regardless of nationality or citizenship. Unfortunately, the U.S. immigration system makes attracting and retaining high-skilled immigrants exceptionally challenging for U.S. firms.

Congress's failure to pass high-skilled immigration reform has exacerbated an already grave situation. For example, the current base cap of 65,000 H-1B visas is arbitrarily set and bears no relation to the U.S. economy's demand for skilled professionals. For fiscal year 2007, the supply ran out more than four months before that fiscal year even began. For fiscal year 2008, the supply of H-1B visas ran out on April 2, 2007, the first day that petitions could be filed and 6 months before the visas would even be issued. Nearly half of those who sought a visa on that day did not receive one.

This situation has caused a serious disruption in the flow of talented STEM graduates to U.S. companies. Because an H-1B petition generally can be filed only for a person who holds a degree, when May/June 2007 graduates received their degrees, the visa cap for fiscal year 2008 had already been reached. Accordingly, U.S. firms will be unable to hire those graduates on an H-1B visa until the beginning of fiscal year 2009, or October 2008.

As a result, many U.S. firms, including Microsoft, have been forced to locate staff in countries that welcome skilled foreign workers to do work that could otherwise have been

Increasing H-1B Visas Would Bring in More Tax Revenue

Raising the H-1B Cap to 195,000 visas will increase income and payroll tax revenues by an estimated $68.8 billion from 2008 to 2016. The government could use these revenues to stimulate economic growth and reduce the trade deficit.

In billions of dollars

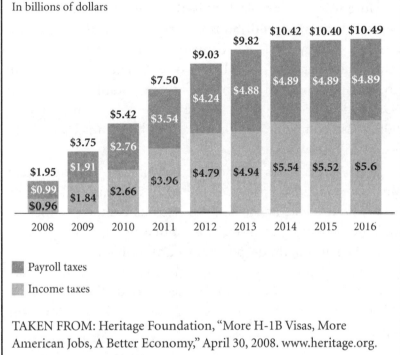

TAKEN FROM: Heritage Foundation, "More H-1B Visas, More American Jobs, A Better Economy," April 30, 2008. www.heritage.org.

done in the United States, if it were not for our counterproductive immigration policies. [In 2007], for example, Microsoft was unable to obtain H-1B visas for one-third of the highly qualified foreign-born job candidates that we wanted to hire.

Boosting All-Around Job Growth

If we increase the number of H-1B visas that are available to U.S. companies, employment of U.S. nationals would likely grow as well. For instance, Microsoft has found that for every

H-1B hire we make, we add on average four additional employees to support them in various capacities. Our experience is not unique. A recent study of technology companies in the S&P 500 [a stock market index] found that, for every H-1B visa requested, these leading U.S. technology companies increased their overall employment by five workers.

Moreover, the simple fact is that highly skilled foreign-born workers make enormous contributions to our economy. A recent survey by Duke University and the University of California—Berkeley found that one quarter of all start-up U.S. engineering and technology firms established between 1995 and 2005 had at least one foreign-born founder. By 2005, these companies produced $52 billion in sales and employed 450,000 workers.

The United States will find it far more difficult to maintain its competitive edge over the next 50 years if it excludes those who are able and willing to help us compete. Other nations are benefiting from our misguided policies. They are revising their immigration policies to attract highly talented students and professionals who would otherwise study, live, and work in the United States for at least part of their careers. To address this problem, I urge Congress to take the following steps.

Streamlining the Visa Process

First, we need to encourage the best students from abroad to enroll in our colleges and universities and, if they wish, to remain in the United States when their studies are completed. One interim step that could be taken would be to extend so-called Optional Practical Training (OPT), the period of employment that foreign students are permitted in connection with their degree program. Students are currently allowed a maximum of 12 months in OPT before they must change their immigration status to continue working in the United States. Extending OPT from 12 to 29 months would help to alleviate the crisis employers are facing due to the current H-1B visa shortage. This only requires action by the Executive Branch, and Congress and this Committee should strongly urge the Department of Homeland Security to take such action immediately.

Second, Congress should create a streamlined path to permanent resident status for highly skilled workers. Rather than allowing highly skilled, well-trained innovators to remain for only a very limited period, we should encourage a greater number to become permanent U.S. residents so that they can help drive innovation and economic growth alongside America's native-born talent. While some foreign students will undoubtedly choose to return home after graduation, it is extremely counterproductive to prevent them from remaining here to contribute their talents and expertise to our economic success if that is what they would like to do.

Third, Congress should increase the cap on visas. The current cap is so low that it virtually assures that highly skilled foreign graduates will leave the United States and work elsewhere after graduation. By increasing the number of visas granted each year, Congress can help U.S. industry meet its near-term need for qualified workers even as we build up our long-term capability to supply these workers domestically through education reform.

To Stay Competitive, America Will Have to Reform

Ultimately, however, if we are to align our immigration policy with global realities and ensure our place as the world's leading innovator, Congress must make additional changes to our employment-based immigration system.

The current system caps employment-based visas—or "green cards"—at 140,000 per fiscal year. Because that number includes spouses and children of applicants, the actual number of visas available for workers is far fewer than 140,000.

Moreover, the number of green cards issued to nationals of any one country cannot exceed 7 percent of the total number of visas issued in a given fiscal year. These two factors have caused multi-year backlogs for thousands of highly skilled individuals and are having a chilling effect on America's ability to attract and retain great talent.

I urge Congress to pass legislation that does away with per-country limits and significantly increases the number of green cards available in any fiscal year. Failure to do so will add to the already years-long wait for green cards and only encourage talented foreign nationals who are already contributing to innovation in U.S. companies to leave and take their talents elsewhere. Innovation is the engine of job growth; if we discourage innovation here at home, economic growth will decline, resulting in fewer jobs for American workers.

I want to emphasize that the shortage of scientists and engineers is so acute that we must do both: reform our education system *and* reform our immigration policies. This is not an either-or proposition. If we do not do both, U.S. companies simply will not have the talent they need to innovate and compete.

"We cannot afford to pursue trade policies that gut our manufacturing sector
and send good jobs overseas."

The Buy American Act Should Be Strengthened

Russ Feingold

*In the following viewpoint, Wisconsin Senator Russ Feingold ar-
gues that the Buy American Act of 1933 needs to be strengthened
in an era of globalization. Because American manufacturers are
losing jobs to overseas competition, Feingold favors the passage of
a Buy American Improvement Act to require that the federal
government make more purchases from domestic suppliers than
foreign suppliers. He claims that too many loopholes allow government purchasers to avoid buying from American firms in favor of cheaper foreign competition. Feingold and his colleague in
the Senate, Sherrod Brown of Ohio, have repeatedly introduced
the Improvement Act in Congress, but the bill has never become
law.*

As you read, consider the following questions:

1. How does Feingold plan to counter the current waiver
   that allows the government to claim that the lowest-

Russ Feingold, Introduction of Legislation to Strengthen Buy American Act, July 29,
2003. http://feingold.senate.gov.

priced domestic bid is "unreasonable" and therefore can be shopped out to cheaper foreign bidders?

2. What is the "micro purchase" waiver that Feingold wants reexamined?

3. By what percentage would Feingold's Improvement Act increase the minimum American-made content standard for government purchases?

Mr. President [of the Senate], today [July 29, 2003] I am introducing legislation to strengthen the Buy American Act of 1933, the statute that governs procurement by the federal government. The name of the act accurately and succinctly describes its purpose: to ensure that the federal government supports domestic companies and domestic workers by buying American-made goods.

While I [am] a strong supporter of the act, I am concerned that, through abuse of its 5 broad waivers, the spirit—if not the letter—of the act is being weakened time and again.

It only makes sense, Mr. President, for the federal government to make every effort to purchase goods that are made in America. A law requiring this common-sense approach should not be necessary. Unfortunately, this law is necessary, and the way in which its many loopholes are being used also makes strengthening it necessary.

America Is Hemorrhaging Jobs

I have often heard my colleagues say on this floor that American-made goods are the best in the world. I could not agree more. This Congress should do more to ensure that the federal government adheres to this sentiment by enforcing and strengthening the provisions of the Buy American Act.

As we all know the United States manufacturing industry is hemorrhaging, as jobs and companies move overseas or are lost altogether. According to the AFL-CIO [American Federation of Labor and Congress of Industrial Organizations], the

United States has lost more than 2.4 million manufacturing jobs since April 1998. This disturbing trend is of particular concern in my home state of Wisconsin.

A March 2003 report by the Wisconsin State Department of Workforce Development notes that "a combination of weak domestic and global demand, mergers and consolidations, automation, globalization of operations, and uncertainty surrounding war have caused employment in Wisconsin's manufacturing sector to shrink in recent years." The Department found that there were 594,100 manufacturing jobs in Wisconsin in 2000, and the Department estimates that this figure had dropped to 517,100 jobs by June of [2003]. More than 77,000 jobs lost in just 2 1/2 years, Mr. President. And the people of my state can expect more of the same during the rest of this decade if we don't take action soon.

While the Department expects some sectors to experience an upturn by 2010, it estimates that the people of my state can still expect to lose thousands more manufacturing jobs by 2010.

Much of this can be blamed on flawed trade agreements that the United States has entered into in recent years. The trade policy of this country over the past several years has been appalling. The trade agreements into which we have entered have contributed to the loss of key employers, ravaging entire communities. But despite that clear evidence, we continue to see trade agreements being reached that will only aggravate this problem.

This has to stop. We cannot afford to pursue trade policies that gut our manufacturing sector and send good jobs overseas. We cannot afford to undermine the protections we have established for workers, the environment, and for our public health and safety. And we cannot afford to squander our democratic heritage by entering into trade agreements that supersede our right to govern ourselves through open, democratic institutions.

I will be introducing legislation in the near future to address that problem directly by establishing minimum standards for the trade agreements into which our nation enters. That measure is a companion to a resolution that will be introduced in the other body by my colleague from Ohio [Mr. [Sherrod] Brown].

The Government Needs to Protect American Business

Regrettably, some of the blame for the dire situation in which American manufacturing finds itself also lies in our own federal tax and procurement policies, some of which actually encourage American companies to move or incorporate abroad. The Buy American law was enacted 70 years ago to ensure that Federal procurement policies support American jobs.

Some argue that the Buy American Act has outlived its usefulness in today's global economy. I argue that it is as relevant today as it was when it was enacted in 1933. The passage of 70 years has not diminished the importance of this Act for American manufacturing companies or for those who are employed in this crucial sector of our economy. In fact, a strong argument can be made that this Act is even more necessary today than it was 70 years ago. With American jobs heading overseas at an alarming rate, the Government should be doing all it can to make sure that U.S. taxpayer dollars are spent to support American jobs.

Some argue that the Buy American Act is protectionist and anti-free trade. I disagree. Supporting American industry is not protectionist—it is common sense. The erosion of our manufacturing base needs to be stopped, and Congress should support procurement and trade policies that help to ensure that we do not continue to lose portions of this vital segment of our economy.

The legislation that I introduce today, the Buy American ~rovement Act, would strengthen the existing Act by tightening existing waivers and would require that information be provided to Congress and to the American people about how often the provisions of this Act are waived by Federal departments and agencies.

Harmful Waivers

As I noted earlier, there are currently five primary waivers in the Buy American Act. The first allows an agency head to waive the Act's provisions if a determination is made that complying with the Act would be "inconsistent with the public interest." I am concerned that this waiver, which includes no definition for what is "inconsistent with the public interest" is actually a gaping loophole that gives broad discretion to department secretaries and agency heads. My bill would clarify this so-called "public interest" waiver provision to prohibit it from being invoked by an agency or department head after a request for procurement (RFP) has been published in the Federal Register. Once the bidding process has begun, the Federal Government should not be able to pull an RFP by saying that it is in the "public interest" to do so. This determination, sometimes referred to as the Buy American Act's national security waiver, should be made well in advance of placing a procurement up for bid.

The Buy American Act may also be waived if the head of the agency determines that the cost of the lowest-priced domestic product is "unreasonable," and a system of price differentials is used to assist in making this determination. My bill would amend this waiver to require that preference be given to the American company if that company's bid is substantially similar to the lowest foreign bid or if the American company is the only domestic source for the item to be procured.

I have a long record of supporting efforts to help taxpayers get the most bang for their buck and of opposing wasteful Federal spending. I don't think anyone can argue that sup-

Evolution of the Buy American Act

The Buy American Act has been transformed by exemptions, additional legislation and legal interpretations throughout its 72-year life. In addition to regional trade agreements, the 1979 Trade Agreements Act supersedes the Buy American Act on contracts with companies from designated countries and worth more than certain amounts (usually $175,000). Instead of focusing only on where products originate, as the Buy American Act does, the Trade Agreements Act also allows products to be "substantially transformed" in an approved country, providing more flexibility. More than 100 items, including rarely used commodities such as rabbit fur and diamonds, are excluded altogether from the law because they are deemed unavailable in the United States. Annual authorization bills often make further exemptions, such as one for information technology products. The rules are even more complicated for Defense: The 1941 Berry Amendment governs the Pentagon's purchases of food and clothing, and agreements with 21 different countries add more exemptions.

Kimberly Palmer, "Buy American,"
Government Executive, *January 1, 2006.*

porting American jobs is "wasteful." We owe it to American manufacturers and their employees to make sure they get a fair shake. I would not support awarding a contract to an American company that is price gouging, but we should make every effort to ensure that domestic sources for goods needed by the Federal Government do not dry up because American ͞mpanies have been slightly underbid by foreign competi-

The Buy American Act also includes a waiver for goods bought by the Federal Government that will be used outside of the United States. There is no question that there will be occasions when the Federal Government will need to procure items quickly that will be used outside the United States, such as in a time of war. However, items that are bought on a regular basis and are used at foreign military bases or United States embassies, for example, could reasonably be procured from domestic sources and shipped to the location where they will be used. My bill would require an analysis of the difference in cost for obtaining articles, materials, or supplies that are used on a regular basis outside the United States, or that are not needed on an immediate basis, from an American company, including the cost of shipping, and a foreign company before issuing a waiver and awarding the contract to a foreign company.

The fourth waiver allowed under the Buy American Act states that the domestic source requirements of the Act may be waived if the articles to be procured are not available from domestic sources "in sufficient and reasonably available commercial quantities and of a satisfactory quality." My bill would require that an agency or department head, prior to issuing such a waiver, conduct a study that determines that domestic production cannot be initiated to meet the procurement needs and that a comparable article, material, or supply is not available from an American company.

The newest Buy American Act waiver, which was enacted in 1994, exempts purchases of less than $2,500 from the domestic source requirements of the Act. While this waiver is not addressed in my bill, I have requested that the General Accounting Office conduct a study of this so-called "micro purchase" exemption, including how often it is used and its impact on American businesses.

Strengthening the Act

My bill also strengthens the Buy American Act in four other ways.

175

First, it expands annual reporting requirements regarding the use of waivers that currently apply only to the Department of Defense to include all Federal departments and agencies. My bill specifies that these reports should include an itemized list of waivers, including the items procured, their dollar value, and their source. In addition, these reports would have to be made available on the Internet.

The bill also increases the minimum American-made content standard for qualification under the Act from the current 50 percent to 75 percent. The definition of what qualifies as an American-made product has been a source of much debate. To me, it seems clear that American-made means manufactured in this country. This classification is a source of pride for manufacturing workers around our country. The current 50 percent standard should be raised to a 75 percent minimum.

My bill also addresses the crucial issue of dual-use technologies and efforts to prevent them from falling into the hands of terrorists or countries of concern. My bill would prohibit the awarding of a contract or sub-contract to a foreign company to manufacture goods containing any item that is classified as a dual-use item on the Commerce Control List unless approval for such a contract has been obtained through the Export Administration Act process.

Finally, my bill would require the General Accounting Office [GAO] to report to Congress with recommendations for defining the terms "inconsistent with the public interest" and "unreasonable cost" for purposes of invoking the corresponding waivers in the Act. I am concerned that both of these terms lack definitions, and that they can be very broadly interpreted by agency or department heads. GAO would be required to make recommendations for statutory definitions of both of these terms, as well as on establishing a consistent waiver process that can be used by all Federal agencies.

I am pleased that this legislation is supported by a broad array of business and labor groups including Save American Manufacturing, the U.S. Business and Industry Council, the International Association of Machinists and Aerospace Workers, the Milwaukee Valve Company, and the National and Wisconsin AFL-CIO.

> "A patchwork of state outsourcing laws would create a complicated, unwieldy framework in which businesses with foreign operations or interests would have to tread."

State Legislation Restricting Outsourcing Is Unconstitutional

Shannon Klinger and M. Lynn Sykes

Shannon Klinger is a lawyer with Alston and Bird. She handles antitrust suits among other litigation. M. Lynn Sykes is an associate with the same firm and works on health care and other public policy matters. In the following viewpoint, Klinger and Sykes argue that recent state legislation aimed at restricting outsourcing is likely to be unconstitutional. Although the Supreme Court has yet to rule on any cases involving this type of legislation, the authors contend that states that attempt to stop private companies (working on state government contracts) from dealing with overseas companies are violating the Foreign Commerce

Shannon Klinger and M. Lynn Sykes, "Exporting the Law: A Legal Analysis of State and Federal Outsourcing Legislation," *National Foundation for American Policy*, April 2004. Reproduced by permission.

Clause. If unchallenged, these laws could jeopardize foreign trade and damage domestic interstate relationships as well, Klinger and Sykes maintain.

As you read, consider the following questions:

1. What are the five factors that Klinger and Sykes believe would lead a U.S. court to strike down anti-outsourcing legislation?
2. According to the authors, what kinds of information transfer do state call center bills commonly try to restrict?
3. How have some legislators tried to couch anti-outsourcing bills as "preference" bills, as the authors explain?

By April 2004, at least 36 states had introduced in excess of 100 bills armed at restricting outsourcing. The National Foundation for American Policy maintains an updated list of such bills and their texts on its Web site. Most of these bills have not yet become law, but at least one has been enacted and the sheer volume of bills seems to indicate that more may become law. State outsourcing legislation generally applies to contracts between private businesses and the state because these contracts, as opposed to contracts between two private companies, are directly under state control. Proposed state legislation also has, however, ventured into regulating the operations of private sector call centers that contact or receive telephone calls from state residents or entities, including centers that send financial, medical, or other data overseas. State outsourcing legislation falls into five general categories. Each category raises preemption and/or constitutional concerns, as discussed in the following [viewpoint]. . . .

Some State Bans Overstep Their Powers

The most legally suspect category of proposed state legislation includes bills that, in general, require that public procurement and other public contracts be performed within the United States. Some states go even further, both restricting the site of contract performance and requiring that only persons authorized to work in the United States perform the contract. Another formulation prohibits a company from receiving state or local contracts, grants, loans, or bonds if the company has had a net loss of employees in the state during the prior calendar year caused by the company relocating jobs from the state to a site that is located outside the United States. To the extent these laws would restrict performance overseas and not in other states, they raise concerns primarily with state-federal relations as opposed to inter-state issues. These concerns include improperly intruding on the federal foreign affairs power and violating the U.S. Constitution's Foreign Commerce Clause. State laws that prohibit the performance of public contracts overseas may be preempted by the Federal Government's power to set uniform policies for the United States as a whole in dealing with foreign nations. The United States Supreme Court has struck down few state statutes as violative of this federal power, but these instances are instructive as we become a "global economy" and states enact laws addressing matters, such as outsourcing, that have a global effect. In a recent case, the Supreme Court ruled that California's Holocaust Victim Insurance Relief Act (HVIRA) impermissibly interfered with the President's conduct of foreign affairs and was preempted on that basis. That law required any insurer doing business in California that sold insurance policies in Europe that were in effect during the Holocaust era to disclose certain information about those policies to the California Insurance Commissioner or risk losing its license. In another ruling, the Court held that an Oregon statute, which stated the conditions under which an alien not residing in the United States could take property in Oregon by succession or testamentary disposition, constituted an improper state intrusion into the field of foreign affairs, an area that the U.S. Constitution entrusts to the President and Congress. The Court reasoned that the statute as applied had "more than 'some incidental or redirect effect in foreign countries'" and "great potential for disruption or embarrassment" and that it "affects international relations in a persistent and subtle way."

This Supreme Court guidance and other federal court decisions reveal that the following factors are likely to lead a court to strike down a state statute as violative of the federal foreign affairs power: (1) the law is designed and intended to affect the affairs of a foreign county; (2) the state "is in a position to effectuate that design and intent and has had an effect"; (3) the effects of the law likely will be magnified if the law at issue should "prove to be a bellwether for other states (and other governments)"; (4) the law has resulted in "serious protests" from other nations, including allies and trading partners, and foreign bodies (such as the European Union); and (5) the state law diverges from federal law, "thus raising the prospect of embarrassment for the country." It is easy to see how state laws prohibiting the performance of public contracts overseas could do all of these things. As a consequence, these laws would likely improperly intrude on the federal foreign affairs power. Though several bills are pending in Congress to set federal policy on outsourcing, current federal foreign policy does not restrict outsourcing as these state laws would. In fact, the President [George W. Bush] and his administration acknowledge that outsourcing is a fact of life in today's global economy, as reflected in [2004-] Secretary of State Colin Powell's remarks during a recent trip to India.

The Dangers of Infringement

A number of courts have emphasized the policy dangers of individual states treading into the foreign affairs realm, affirming the shaky legal footing of state laws wholesale restricting public contracts from being performed overseas. [The U.S. courts have said,] "These are delicate matters. If state action could defeat or alter our foreign policy, serious consequences might ensue. The nation as a whole would be held to answer if a state created difficulties with a foreign power." A state cannot "structure national foreign policy to conform to its own domestic policies." Accordingly, "[a]ny concurrent state power that may exist [in the area of international relations] is restricted to the narrowest of limits. . . ." Although most authority is to the contrary, not all state laws affecting foreign commerce have been found to run afoul of the federal foreign affairs power. Lower courts are split on the constitutionality of state Buy American Acts, and the Supreme Court has not ruled definitively on the issue. . . .

The Foreign Commerce Clause protects American companies acting outside the geographic borders of the United States. [A federal court ruled,] "When the Constitution speaks of foreign commerce, it is not referring only to attempts to regulate the conduct of foreign companies; it is also referring to attempts to restrict the actions of American companies overseas." State laws that prohibit the performance of public contracts internationally would preclude U.S. interest overseas from working on state contracts. The Supreme Court subjects state laws that affect foreign commerce to a higher level of scrutiny than those affecting only domestic commerce. . . .

As in the area of Federal foreign affairs power, the Supreme Court considers the effect of other states enacting similar laws. "If other States followed the taxing State's example, various instrumentalities of commerce could be subjected to varying degrees of multiple taxation, a result that would plainly prevent this Nation from speaking with one voice in regulating foreign commerce." A patchwork of state outsourcing laws would create a complicated, unwieldy framework in which businesses with foreign operations or interests would have to tread. Another consideration under both a foreign affairs powers and Foreign Commerce Clause analysis is the possibility of retaliation by foreign nations. The Supreme

State Laws Passed on Offshore Outsourcing, 2005

California–AB 1741 prohibits voter information from being sent outside the United States. Signed by Governor on July 25, 2005.

Colorado–HB 1307 provides an in-state preference for agricultural products and prohibits Governor from binding state on future trade agreements. Signed by Governor on June 7, 2005.

Illinois–S 1723 provides a preference of items manufactured in the United States for procurement purposes. Signed by Governor on August 10, 2005.

Maryland–HB 514 prohibits Governor from binding state on future trade agreements. Legislature voted to override Governor's veto of bill on April 11, 2005.

New Jersey–S 494 prohibits state contract work from being performed outside the United States. Signed by Governor on May 5, 2005. *Note: This law represents the most restrictive anti-outsourcing legislation in the nation.*

North Carolina–HB 800 requires a vendor submitting a bid to disclose "where services will be performed under the contract," including performance outside the United States. Signed by Governor July 7, 2005.

North Dakota–H 1091 provides an in-state preference on equal bids on state contracts. Signed by Governor on March 30, 2005.

National Foundation for American Policy, 2005.
www.nfap.com.

Court has also noted that, at times: "[r]etaliation by some na-tions could be automatic" due to statutes requiring reciprocity in trade matters. Given that as of 2001, over 6.4 million Americans were employed directly by foreign corporations doing business in the United States, foreign retaliation could have a substantial effect on the American economy. . . .

Restricting State Jobs to U.S. Employees Intrudes on Foreign Affairs

Another related category of state bills requires that state contracts be performed by individuals who are United States citizens or authorized to work in the United States. Some proposed legislation incorporates these provisions into call center restriction bills to restrict the status of call center employees. Other bills restrict employment in performing any state contract.

These bills, as with bills restricting the location of work to be performed under state contracts, may improperly intrude on the federal foreign affairs power and violate the Foreign Commerce Clause. Note that a United States citizen working abroad would be eligible to work on public contracts for states that prohibit the work from being done by individuals who are not United States citizens or authorized to work in the United States but would be ineligible to work on public contracts for states that prohibit the work from being done overseas. This scenario is just one example of the myriad of complications that will arise in applying these varied state outsourcing provisions. Whether the drafters thought these issues through is unknown.

Other Tactics to Restrict Outsourcing

State call center bills generally provide that individuals receiving telephone calls from or placing calls to customer sales or service centers have the right to certain information about the call center employees with whom they are speaking, such as the location of the call center employee, the employee's place of business, and the name of the employee. A number of these bills also prohibit customer sales or service centers from sending certain financial or personal identifying information to a foreign country without the express written consent of the customer.

Some proposed legislation both prohibits the state from contracting for telemarketing or telephone center services with any vendor employing the services of persons not authorized to work in the United States and requires that the call center services be performed in the United States. Another variation, in the case of private sector call centers, gives the caller or called party the right to be transferred to a contact center in the United States upon request, apparently presuming that a caller would rather speak with someone in the United States than overseas. Although these call center restrictions do not raise significant constitutional concerns on their face, they may nonetheless, as applied, implicate the federal foreign affairs power and the Foreign Commerce Clause.

Proponents of proposed limitations on the ability of corporations to utilize offshore call centers or otherwise avail themselves of outsourcing when medical, financial, or other personal data is involved often do so under the justification that the restrictions are necessary in order to protect the privacy interests of the American public. As Rep. Edward J. Markey (D-MA) [has] stated: "in their rush to cut costs and increase their bottom line . . . companies may be sacrificing the privacy protections the law affords to American citizens by transferring sensitive information to offshore companies that are outside of the reach of U.S. privacy law beyond the jurisdiction of U.S. regulators."

The legal basis for such alarmist concerns is questionable. First, . . . the United States is subject to a variety of trade obligations, including its obligations under the World Trade Organization's (WTO) Agreement on Government Procurement (GPA). An outright ban on the global sourcing of, among other things, call center functions, medical records transcription, or the processing of financial transactions would likely run afoul of one or more such trade agreements.

Second, such an argument fails to appreciate that Congress has already passed a number of federal laws aimed at protecting consumer privacy, including the Fair Credit Reporting Act, the Health Insurance Portability and Accountability Act of 1996 (HIPAA), and the Gramm-Leach-Bliley Act of 1999 (GLB). Each of these statutes contains provisions that may preempt in whole or in part efforts undertaken by the various states to limit the global sourcing of personal information. . . .

Preferential Treatment Bills Are Discriminatory

Some bills—and a new state law—couch local favoritism as preferences, rather than as outright requirements or prohibitions. The most striking example is a new Indiana law, which will go into effect on July 1, 2004. This law offers price preferences of between one and five percent to Indiana companies in awarding state contracts. The law also contains a reciprocal benefit carve-out, which provides that the preference does not apply to the detriment of businesses from states bordering Indiana if the bordering states do not provide purchasing preferences to their businesses more favorable than preferences provided to Indiana businesses under the law. Other states have bills or executive orders with similar preferences for in-state businesses. A related type of proposed legislation prohibits private companies from receiving state or local contracts, grants, loans, or bonds if they have had a loss of employees in the state caused by the relocation of jobs from the state to a site that is located outside of the United States.

Preferential treatment bills are on their face discriminatory. While not an outright prohibition on outsourcing, their restrictions operate largely to the same effect. Potential constitutional problems with preferential treatment bills focus on the relationship among states and include potential violations of the Commerce Clause, the Privileges and Immunities Clause, and principles of Full Faith and Credit.

There are sound reasons to believe that state preferential treatment laws may violate the Commerce Clause, which, in addition to providing for Congress's power to regulate commerce with foreign nations, establishes Congress's power to "regulate Commerce . . . among the several States."

States Cannot Control Business Beyond Their Borders

States generally may not regulate commerce outside their borders. "The critical inquiry is whether the practical effect of the regulation is to control conduct beyond the boundaries of the State," [the courts have said.] "Generally speaking, the Commerce Clause protects against inconsistent legislation arising from the projection of one state regulatory regime into the jurisdiction of another State. . . ."

In almost any Commerce Clause case, including in the outsourcing context, a state can argue that it has an interest in supporting local businesses and employment. "Yet these arguments are at odds with the general principle that the Commerce Clause prohibits a State from using its regulatory power to protect its own citizens from outside competition," [the courts maintain.] State preferential treatment laws would attempt to do just that.

In conducting this Commerce Clause analysis, [the court ruled,] "the practical effect of the statute must be evaluated not only by considering the consequences of the statute itself, but also by considering how the challenged statute may interact with the legitimate regulatory regimes of other States and what effect would arise if not one, but many or every, State adopted similar legislation." As in the international context, a patchwork of state outsourcing laws would create a complex, strained environment for inter-state relations.

Periodical Bibliography

The following articles have been selected to supplement the diverse views presented in this chapter.

Clive Crook	"Beyond Trade Adjustment Assistance," *National Journal*, July 28, 2007.
Darren Dahl	"States Target Outsourcing," *Inc.*, July 2004.
Peter Elstrom	"Work Visas May Work Against the U.S.," *Business Week*, February 8, 2007.
Adam Graham-Silverman	"TAA Bill Would Help Workers Whose Jobs Are Lost to Foreign Competition," *CQ Weekly*, November 5, 2007.
Moira Herbst	"Guess Who's Getting the Most Work Visas," *Business Week*, March 17, 2008.
Tim Kane and Daniella Markheim	"TAA Reform Is Not Enough," *WebMemo*, no. 1574, July 30, 2007. www.heritage.org.
Marianne Kolbasuk McGee and Alice LaPlante	"Talent Search," *Information Week*, July 23, 2007.
Marianne Kolbasuk McGee and Chris Murphy	"Do Indian Outsourcers Misuse the H-1B Visa Programs?" *Information Week*, May 21, 2007.
Shawn Zeller	"Certified Outsourcing," *CQ Weekly*, May 28, 2007.

OPPOSING
VIEWPOINTS®
SERIES

CHAPTER 4

What Is the Global Impact of Outsourcing?

Chapter Preface

Outsourcing has had a cultural impact on many countries, and India is no exception. While the effects of outsourcing do not often reach the villages and countrysides in India, its effects in cities have been remarkable. Wages have gone up in these areas, and more Indians are able to afford luxury items such as cars and cell phones. In addition, some businesses—such as call centers—are set up on a U.S. model built around work culture, day-to-day business practices, and even U.S. holiday recognition. This model has transformed Indian life for many urban Indians.

Adapting to American models is not the only transformation brought on by increased job opportunities. For example, the role of women has changed drastically in India. Women, who before the outsourcing boom occupied a small percentage of the workforce, now make up a large percentage of the Indian workforce. Mobile phone provider Nokia states that 70 percent of its Indian workforce is female. This is allegedly because "women pass our dexterity test better than male walk-ins," says Sachin Saxena, a director of operations and logistics at Nokia. Sunder Vadivel of Perlos, another mobile phone provider, claims that "women get employed not by deliberate design. It's just that they are eminently suited for the telecom manufacturing industry or wherever electronic components are used." Indian women's newfound empowerment in these realms has allowed them to become more financially independent in a society that is traditionally patriarchal.

Outsourcing to India, however, has not only impacted the business sector. Indian women are also involved in the outsourcing of childbirth—an unusual practice, but one that pays well. A small clinic at Kaival Hospital in Anand, for example, matches young Indian women with infertile couples from countries such as Britain and the United States. The clinic then impregnates the surrogate through in vitro fertilization. The surrogate lives at the clinic, is cared for during the pregnancy, and is offered counseling after she delivers the couple's baby. Women are paid in the range of $4,500 to $6,500 for this service—a relatively large sum of money for most Indians. The foreign couples generally pay less than a total of $10,000 for their child. The practice is becoming more accepted in India, where it has been legal since 2002. But resistance to this form of outsourcing reveals how the liberalizing effects of global trade can still run against moral and cultural opposition at times.

In the following chapter, Audrey Carpio comments on cultural changes that have occurred in the Philippines as a result of outsourcing. Other authors in the chapter discuss various impacts of outsourcing on global economies and the concerns American investors have in placing their business interests in such rapidly transforming regions.

"*To maintain its growth, India clearly will have to speed up . . . infrastructure improvements.*"

Lack of Infrastructure Is Hampering India's Outsourcing Industry

Rebecca Fannin

Rebecca Fannin is the international editor of the Hong Kong weekly Asian Venture Capital Journal. *Since 1992, she has been reporting on innovation, technology, and the emerging economies in Hong Kong, Bangalore, Singapore, Beijing, Shanghai, and other major cities around the world. In the following viewpoint, Fannin claims that poorly developed infrastructure is hampering India's ability to fully take advantage of outsourcing opportunities. She contends that India's utilities have still not modernized to keep up with technological progress, and road networks are still primitive in many areas. She even notes how India's information technology workforce lacks many skills that foreign competitors possess. She stipulates that further improvement is necessary for India to maintain its outsourcing edge.*

As you read, consider the following questions:

1. According to Fannin, about how many hours of electricity a day do Bangalore businesses receive?
2. In the author's view, what advantages does India have over China as an outsourcing location?
3. How much does Azim Premji believe India's outsourcing could increase by 2009?

The bumpy roads leading to Bangalore's Electronics City are thronged with rickshaws, overcrowded buses, mopeds, noisy old trucks, ox-drawn carts of fruit and lumber—even the occasional cow ambling along, ignoring the blare of honking horns. Trash is strewn along the road, which is lined with aluminum shacks.

In stark contrast to the chaotic street scene, are numerous cybercafés and neon-lit pubs, filled with software engineers drinking Kingfisher beer. Once known as a "garden city" and a "pensioner's paradise" for its temperate climate and greenery, Bangalore is today a Silicon Valley [a region in Northern California known for its high concentration of high-tech businesses] of India, home to leading outsourcing companies, Wipro and Infosys Technologies, as well as numerous Western corporations such as General Electric and Philips.

The sprawling corporate campuses of India's third-party vendors have tennis courts, golf carts for transportation, swimming pools, open-air cafeterias, waterfalls, palm trees, too many cell phones, smoking areas, training centers, health clubs, polished granite lobbies and videoconferencing facilities. The gaps between corporate headquarter locations and surrounding areas is so stark that Indians refer to company campuses as "islands."

Summing up the contrast, Raman Roy, president of Wipro Spectramind, notes: "The common impression of India is of people going to work on a bullock cart while they talk on their cell phone."

That picture has stirred a roiling debate over just how many more jobs India—arguably the world's current outsourcing capital—can absorb in the realms of both business process and information technology [IT]. On one side of the debate, skeptics argue that India's ancient and sagging infrastructure places an inherent limit on how many jobs can move here. On the other side, optimists believe the vast numbers of educated, skilled and willing workers means India can absorb hundreds of thousands of more jobs.

Outsourcing Boom

To be sure, the recent growth of India's outsourcing sector, now worth $12 billion a year in sales, has been nothing short of spectacular. The ... business process outsourcing (BPO) segment, made up of customer-service call centers and administrative facilities handling airline reservations, mortgage applications and insurance claims, is projected to grow by 54 percent ... [in 2007], to $3.6 billion, on top of a 59 percent growth rate ... [in 2003], according to the National Association of Software and Service Companies (NASSCOM) [the premier organization that represents and sets the tone for public policy for the Indian software industry]. The more than decade-old information technology services and products industry is forecast to increase 17 percent, to $8.4 billion, after an 18 percent jump the year before, according to NASSCOM, which pegs the number of IT professionals at 650,000, up dramatically from 6,800 in 1985. By 2008, the Indian outsourcing market will reach $77 billion with 2 million employees, up from 770,000 currently, predicts McKinsey & Co.

But there are numerous threats to India's continued dominance in outsourcing. While telecommunications have improved considerably with cell phones, satellite transmissions and trans-oceanic fiber optic cable, most other utilities and services have not been updated. Electric power is so unreliable that Wipro Spectramind and other corporations have backup generators. "We are lucky to get 15 hours of electricity daily from the government," says Roy. Many firms have their own water supply, too.

A new highway under construction, called the Golden Quadrilateral and linking Mumbai, New Delhi, Chennai, Kolkata and other Indian cities, won't be completed for a couple of years. It takes an hour to travel 20 kilometers (12 miles) on Bangalore's congested roads to reach the city's outsourcing hubs in Electronics City and Whitefield. Construction of a new international airport to open up more direct flights to Bangalore from cities in Europe and the U.S. hasn't begun. Hotel reservations at the luxurious Taj West End and the trendy Leela Palace are hard to get, and few new hotels are being built. While there has been much talk about an elevated railway for Bangalore, so far it's only talk. And with no mass transit option yet, most corporations have to bus their employees to and from work.

India's Edge on China

Aside from India's poor infrastructure, there is international competition, a dearth of workers with managerial skills to fill mid-level jobs, and turnover rates of as high as 50 percent among entry-level workers in the back-office services industry. In terms of emerging competitors for outsourcing business, China is an IT stronghold, the Philippines is a base for bilingual Spanish-English language skill and Eastern Europe is a customer service center for Europe. Even Wipro Spectramind, India's leading provider of outsourced business processes, is going abroad, adding a 200-person development center in Shanghai and a Czech Republic branch to handle European customers.

In an analysis of outsourcing locations, the Gartner Group puts India ahead of China in language skills, government support, labor pool, costs, educational system, cultural compatibility and data/IP [intellectual property] security. The only

Infrastructure Woes

With virtually no mass transit in Bangalore, Indian technology firm Infosys Technologies Ltd. spends $5 million a year on buses, minivans, and taxis to transport its 18,000 employees to and from Electronics City. And traffic jams mean workers can spend upwards of four hours commuting each day. "India has underinvested in infrastructure for 60 years, and we're behind what we need by 10 to 12 years," says T.V. Mohandas Pai, director of human resources for Infosys. . . .

[India's] economic boom is being built on the shakiest of foundations. Highways, modern bridges, world-class airports, reliable power, and clean water are in desperately short supply. And what's already there is literally crumbling under the weight of progress. In December [2006], a bridge in eastern India collapsed, killing 34 passengers in a train rumbling underneath. Economic losses from congestion and poor roads alone are as high as $6 billion a year, says Gajendra Haldea, an adviser to the federal Planning Commission. . . .

Steve Haman, "The Trouble with India,"
Business Week, March 19, 2007. www.businessweek.com.

areas where China outperforms India are infrastructure and political stability. "China has made tremendous progress and for India to fulfill its potential it needs work on new roads, hotels, water supply, air transport and mass transit," says Infosys CEO Nandan Nilekani from his informal, working office at the company's sprawling 70-acre headquarters in Electronics City.

So far, managing the sheer speed of growth has been the most challenging part of Nilekani's job. Infosys is eyeing revenues of $1 billion for the fiscal year ending March 2004, up from $753 million the year before and from $121 million in 1999, "during the rockiest time in the IT world," he says. "When we founded this company, we didn't visualize this kind of dimension—the enormity of what is possible," Nilekani says.

Continued growth in outsourcing business faces another significant hurdle: the political outcry over the loss of U.S. jobs. "A backlash has developed in the run-up to the elections," notes Nilekani, "but frankly we believe the world operates on a free trade basis and you trade on what you are good at." Ultimately, U.S. companies see improved productivity and stronger financials as a result, he says, and that will lead to increased U.S. exports to India companies.

The sentiment among outsourcing leaders is that the political controversy will subside once the elections are over, and that the "noise" is out of proportion to the issue. For instance, Forrester Research estimates that 300,000 U.S. jobs have been lost to outsourcing, of a total 2.7 million U.S. job losses. . . .

Backlash aside, [Azam] Premji [the chairman and managing director at Wipro] remains sanguine about India's ability to accommodate more jobs. "Infrastructure? Of course it's a problem," says the CEO. . . . But he points to rapid telecommunications improvements and a speedup of road, bridges and ports construction with government liberalization. Upcoming privatization in the power industry within four years should put the "power issues behind us," adds Premji, who is considered the Bill Gates of India for his fortune in Wipro shares, which are listed on the New York Stock Exchange.

To maintain its growth, India clearly will have to speed up those infrastructure improvements. Bangalore is one of the more modern cities in India, but by comparison, Shanghai—a key rival—looks like it belongs on another futuristic planet, with its mag-lev [magnetic levitation] elevated railway, efficient subway system, new international airport, steady power supplies and well-engineered roads and bridges. Domestic rivalry within India, meanwhile, is keeping the pressure on. Bangalore vies for business with Hyderabad in the south and with the New Delhi suburbs of Noida and Gurgaon in the north. Pune, Chennai and Kolkata are also becoming contenders.

Assuming improvements continue, Premji believes India could easily see outsourcing growth of 20 to 25 percent [from 2007 to 2009]. Wipro saw revenues climb 44 percent to $343 million in the third quarter ending December 2003 compared with the same period a year earlier while net income grew 22 percent, to $58 million. . . .

The Need for Continued Improvement

One pleased client among Wipro's 300 customers is Blackwell Book Services, a division of the British bookseller. Two years ago, it hired a small Wipro software group to help supplement its 20-person software team in Portland, Ore. "The quality of the work is very sound," says Cloy Swartzendruber, Blackwell's vice president of IT [information technology]. "You get exactly what you ask for—and then some," he says. The team in India has specialized skills in working with IBM [International Business Machines Corporation] mainframes that their U.S. counterparts lack, at one-half to one-third the cost of U.S. engineers. Even so, he stresses that no one in the U.S. office has lost their job to the Indian software team, although some work has dropped off with U.S. consulting firms.

There's plenty of room for India's outsourcing sector to attract more customers from abroad. India claims only 2 percent of the $180 billion software products market worldwide, according to NASSCOM. In BPO, however, India already claims a dominant 80 percent of the global market.

Most booms don't last forever, though, and Gartner research vice president Rita Terdiman says Indian outsourcing should reach maturity by 2007. Already, consolidation is occurring. "The big are getting bigger and most clients want to go with one vendor and one brand name," says Nilekani. McKinsey partner Jayant Sinha argues that one or two major global players with lower-cost and value-added services will dominate the business.

The single biggest question revolves around labor. India's labor pool stands at 470 million people, with 9 million new entrants each year. Incredibly, Infosys claims to have received 1 million applications . . . [in 2003] for 9,000 new jobs. While software programming prowess abounds, managerial experience is thin. "We have to bring managers in from overseas or hire them from other industries," says Akshaya Bhargava, CEO of Progeon, a BPO partnership with Infosys.

Training a steady influx of workers is a big job. Wipro has an on-site "university" with 70 full-time faculty who train 2,500 new yearly recruits for 35 days and teach management skills and software programming courses. Students get reimbursed for the coursework when they pass certification tests.

At call centers, getting inquiries resolved on the first attempt is a key goal. Roy says his firm has seen a 40- to 50-percent improvement in "first-time resolution" over . . . [2003] and adds, "eight out of 10 people don't call back."

But high turnover of 50 percent-plus at most centers is a challenge. Causing that turnover are everything from night shifts answering calls from strangers on the other side of the globe, disillusionment with a mundane routine, few opportunities for advancement and higher salary offers from rivals. "We have to position BPO as not just fun, but a long-term career," says Progeon's Bhargava, who adds that industry specialization could be one way to relieve the monotony and offer career advancement. . . .

India's Advantage Is Its Human Capital

Multinational companies such as American Express, Standard Chartered and Citigroup also are having to grapple with these issues as their numbers multiply, increasing to 32 percent of the Indian outsourcing market . . . [in 2003], up from 26 percent in 2002.

Dutch electronics company Philips maintains a huge R&D [research and development] center in Bangalore, with some 1,150 software engineers to design chips for all of Philips DVDs and some other electronic devices. The labs are the biggest among Philips' 25 R&D centers employing 2,000 overall, says Philips Software CEO Bob Hoekstra. The Indian group claims 23 patents and has saved Philips 100 million Euros in product development costs since it started . . . says Hoekstra. Salaries are 50 percent to 70 percent lower than in the U.S. or Europe and there is no shortage of engineer applicants, he adds. "I could think of 1,000 reasons that we would fail with this offshore operation," says Hoekstra. "But the engineers here have a keen ability to stretch themselves and they have a high level of motivation."

Likewise, Indian CEOs argue that the quality of their labor pool will overcome all the other challenges. "When CEOs come here from abroad and look under the hood, they are absolutely amazed," says Nilekani, looking out over a room filled with fresh-faced software engineers debating the finer points of programming code. "The thing that is winning this for India is the human capital," he adds. If he's right, jobs will keep moving to India—for many years to come.

> "To beat back emerging rivals, Indian companies are hiring workers and opening offices in developing countries themselves, before their clients do."

India Is Outsourcing Outsourcing

Anand Giridharadas

Anand Giridharadas writes about Indian affairs for the International Herald Tribune *and the* New York Times. *His subjects are business, culture, and globalization. In the following viewpoint, Giridharadas claims that outsourcing has become such a growing industry in India that Indian corporations are forced to outsource jobs to developing nations to meet the need for workers who speak the varieties of languages that global clients demand. As Giridharadas explains, Indian service companies are exporting their experience to foreign shores where they can gather low-wage workers who can deal with the language requirements of specific users.*

As you read, consider the following questions:

1. What are some of the foreign nations in which Indian information technology businesses are opening offices?

2. According to Giridharadas, what does the company Infosys say it has learned from its outsourcing experience in India?

3. As the author explains, why does Infosys choose to hire novices to work in its foreign offices?

Thousands of Indians report to Infosys Technologies' campus ... [in Mysore, India] to learn the finer points of programming. Lately, though, packs of foreigners have been roaming the manicured lawns, too.

Many of them are recent American college graduates, and some have even turned down job offers from coveted employers like Google. Instead, they accepted a novel assignment from Infosys, the Indian technology giant: fly here for six months of training, then return home to work in the company's American back offices.

India is outsourcing outsourcing.

One of the constants of the global economy has been companies moving their tasks—and jobs—to India. But rising wages and a stronger currency here, demands for workers who speak languages other than English, and competition from countries looking to emulate India's success as a back office—including China, Morocco and Mexico—are challenging that model.

Many executives here acknowledge that outsourcing, having rained most heavily on India, will increasingly sprinkle tasks around the globe. Or, as Ashok Vemuri, an Infosys senior vice president, put it, the future of outsourcing is "to take the work from any part of the world and do it in any part of the world."

To fight on the shifting terrain, and to beat back emerging rivals, Indian companies are hiring workers and opening offices in developing countries themselves, before their clients do.

The New Outsourcing

In May [2007], Tata Consultancy Service, Infosys's Indian rival, announced a new back office in Guadalajara, Mexico; Tata already has 5,000 workers in Brazil, Chile and Uruguay. Cognizant Technology Solutions, with most of its operations in India, has now opened back offices in Phoenix and Shanghai.

Wipro, another Indian technology services company, has outsourcing offices in Canada, China, Portugal, Romania and Saudi Arabia, among other locations.

And . . . Wipro said it was opening a software development center in Atlanta that would hire 500 programmers in three years.

In a poetic reflection of outsourcing's new face, Wipro's chairman, Azim Premji, told Wall Street analysts this year that he was considering hubs in Idaho and Virginia, in addition to Georgia, to take advantage of American "states which are less developed." (India's per capita income is less than $1,000 a year.)

For its part, Infosys is building a whole archipelago of back offices—in Mexico, the Czech Republic, Thailand and China, as well as low-cost regions of the United States.

The company seeks to become a global matchmaker for outsourcing: any time a company wants work done somewhere else, even just down the street, Infosys wants to get the call.

It is a peculiar ambition for a company that symbolizes the flow of tasks from the West to India.

Most of Infosys's 75,000 employees are Indians, in India. They account for most of the company's $3.1 billion in sales

"Our salaries are so low, companies in India are outsourcing to us." Cartoon by Harley Schwadron. www.CartoonStock.com.

in the year that ended March 31 [2007], from work for clients like Bank of America and Goldman Sachs.

"India continues to be the No. 1 location for outsourcing," S. Gopalakrishnan, the company's chief executive, said in a telephone interview.

And yet the company opened a Philippines office in August and, a month earlier, bought back offices in Thailand and Poland from Royal Philips Electronics, the Dutch company. In each outsourcing hub, local employees work with little help from Indian managers.

Dividing up Tasks Across the Globe

Infosys says its outsourcing experience in India has taught it to carve up a project, apportion each slice to suitable workers, double-check quality and then export a final, reassembled product to clients. The company argues it can clone its Indian back offices in other nations and groom Chinese, Mexican or Czech employees to be more productive than local outsourcing companies could make them.

"We have pioneered this movement of work," Mr. Gopalakrishnan said. "These new countries don't have experience and maturity in doing that, and that's what we're taking to these countries."

Some analysts compare the strategy to Japanese penetration of auto manufacturing in the United States in the 1970s. Just as the Japanese learned to make cars in America without Japanese workers, Indian vendors are learning to outsource without Indians, said Dennis McGuire, chairman of TPI, a Texas-based outsourcing consultancy.

Though work that bypasses India remains a small part of the Infosys business, it is growing. The company can be highly secretive, but executives agreed to describe some of the new projects on the condition that clients not be identified.

In one project, an American bank wanted a computer system to handle a loan program for Hispanic customers. The system had to work in Spanish. It also had to take into account variables particular to Hispanic clients: many, for instance, remit money to families abroad, which can affect their bank balances. The bank thought a Mexican team would have the right language skills and grasp of cultural nuances.

But instead of going to a Mexican vendor, or to an American vendor with Mexican operations, the bank retained three dozen engineers at Infosys, which had recently opened shop in Monterrey, Mexico.

Looking to India Instead of Closer Vendors

Such is the new outsourcing: A company in the United States pays an Indian vendor 7,000 miles away to supply it with Mexican engineers working 150 miles south of the United States border.

In Europe, too, companies now hire Infosys to manage back offices in their own backyards. When an American manufacturer, for instance, needed a system to handle bills from multiple vendors supplying its factories in different European countries, it turned to the Indian company. The manufacturer's different locations scan the invoices and send them to an office of Infosys, where each bill is passed to the right language team. The teams verify the orders and send the payment to the suppliers while logged in to the client's computer system.

More than a dozen languages are spoken at the Infosys office, which is in Brno, Czech Republic.

The American program here in Mysore is meant to keep open that pipeline of diversity.

Most trainees here have no software knowledge. By teaching novices, Infosys saves money and hopes to attract workers who will turn down better-known companies for the chance to learn a new skill.

"It's the equivalent of a bachelor's in computer science in six months," said Melissa Adams, a 22-year-old trainee. Ms. Adams graduated . . . from the University of Washington with a business degree, and rejected Google for Infosys.

And yet, even as outsourcing takes on new directions, old perceptions linger.

For instance, when Jeff Rand, a 23-year-old American trainee, told his grandmother he was moving to India to work as a software engineer for six months, "she said, 'Maybe I'll get to talk to you when I have a problem with my credit card.'"

Said Mr. Rand with a rueful chuckle, "It took me about two or three weeks to explain to my grandma that I was not going to be working in a call center."

| *"China is a convenient bogeyman for all sorts of ills and fears."*

China Has Become a Scapegoat for American Outsourcing Fears

Zachary Karabell

In the following viewpoint, Zachary Karabell argues that Americans unfairly blame China for producing shoddy—sometimes dangerous—goods. Karabell asserts that the backlash against China has more to do with its stature as an economic competitor with proven infrastructure and production capabilities. Karabell maintains that companies, not countries, should be responsible for the quality of the products that they put on the market. Zachary Karabell is the executive vice president for Fred Alger Management. He is also the author of several books, and his essays and reviews have appeared in the New York Times, Los Angeles Times, Foreign Policy, *and* Newsweek.

As you read, consider the following questions:

1. According to Karabell, why is China an appealing location for outsourcing?

2. How does Karabell put the issue of safety-recalls in context?

3. What are the "legitimate" demands that America can make on China, in Karabell's view?

The recent outcry over poisonous pet food and the recall of lead-tainted toys sourced by Mattel in China proves one thing: We have a China problem. It is not, however, a China problem in the way most people think. It is not a problem with safety standards that threaten our children and our pets. It is a problem with the very fact of China as an emerging force on the global economic stage, and it underscores a profound and worrying trend in American political and economic life. For half a century we fought for the creation of a global capitalist system. Now that we have one, we seem to have forgotten one little thing: Capitalism means competition, and we are acting like we can't handle it.

To understand that the uproar over the toys isn't really about product safety, we need to look back at the past few years and see that the current hullabaloo is just the latest incarnation of our simmering China problem.

Putting Pressure on China

The rumblings began during the election of 2004, with accusations that U.S. companies that outsourced work to China were traitorous and being led by "Benedict Arnold CEOs." Never mind that most of the jobs outsourced to China had already been outsourced to Mexico a decade ago. The chorus grew ... [in 2005], when one of China's state-owned energy companies attempted to buy Unocal. That led to a strenuous and yes, bipartisan, position in Congress that allowing the deal to go forward would jeopardize national security and unfairly benefit China. Democratic Sen. Ron Wyden declared: "I don't think being a free-trader is synonymous with being a sucker and patsy." The Republicans were no better. The deal was scuttled.

Then ... [in 2006], the sharply rising trade deficit and current account deficit with China generated pressure in Congress to force China to allow its currency (the yuan) to appreciate more rapidly against the U.S. dollar. The first proposal was sponsored by Sens. Lindsey Graham and Charles Schumer and would slap China with a 27.5% tariff unless it allows for an immediate and sharp revaluation. The second is working through the Senate this summer [2007] and is sponsored by Sens. Charles Grassley and Max Baucus. It would force the Treasury Department to label China a currency manipulator based on the fact that China doesn't allow the yuan to float freely. That in turn would lead to series of procedural moves with escalating penalties.

Never mind the fact that even a substantial rise in the currency wouldn't change the dynamics of U.S.-China trade. China is appealing not just because of costs but because of a reliable infrastructure and a proven ability to produce. Never mind that sourcing in China has direct benefits for hundreds of millions of Americans in the form of less expensive goods, from appliances to entertainment. Never mind that China partly subsidizes U.S. spending and consumption by purchasing hundreds of billions of dollars worth of U.S. Treasuries. And never mind that China has become an integral market for U.S. goods and companies, as the purchasing power of Chinese consumers rises rapidly. Macau is already a larger market for U.S. gaming companies than Las Vegas, and multinationals such as Proctor & Gamble and GE [General Electric] are seeing some of their fastest, most substantial growth from selling to China, not from sourcing in China.

While the rhetoric in Congress ... isn't likely to derail these trends, the unwillingness to acknowledge the benefits of China's rise is part of a pattern of China bashing that raises questions about the ability of the U.S. to compete in the global economy that it did so much to create.

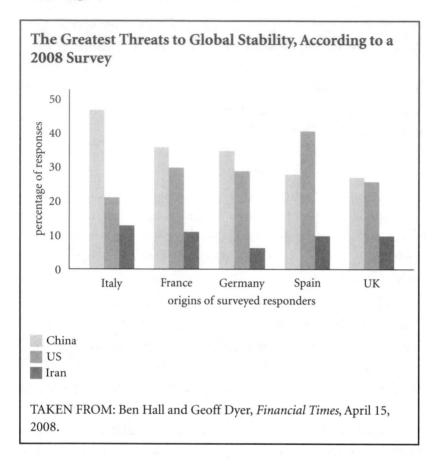

The Greatest Threats to Global Stability, According to a 2008 Survey

TAKEN FROM: Ben Hall and Geoff Dyer, *Financial Times*, April 15, 2008.

Companies, Not Countries, Are Responsible for Products

The issue of safety needs to be seen in this context. There is no question that standards in China are less rigorous than they should be. But consumer concerns over product safety long predate the current scare, and only a severe case of amnesia can turn this into a China issue. Remember Ralph Nader in his 1960s heyday? How about the global recall of Perrier water (made in France) in 1990 because of fears of benzene contamination? Or the rollover problem of the Ford Explorer in the same period? What about the recall of halogen torchier lamps in 1997 because of an unfortunate tendency for the bulbs to explode?

Read the annual report of the U.S. Consumer Product Safety Commission in 1990, which pointed to the recall of infant "bean bag" cushions made in the U.S. that caused 30 deaths. Moreover, given the recent outcry over dangerous tires made in China, we should remember that this pales in comparison to the 88 deaths attributed to defective Firestone Tires in the late 1990s that led to the recall of 6.5 million in 2000.

This is only a small sample of product recalls in the past 20 years that had nothing to do with China. While ... China is a major source of product defects, the actual number of faulty products is, regrettably, normal—proportionate to how much it produces and comparable to the safety issues that have bedeviled manufacturers of all nationalities in past decades. Companies, not countries, bear ultimate responsibility for what they sell under the label, and it says something about current attitudes that so many have collectively forgotten the recent history of product safety concerns and turned it into a China problem.

Chinese officials recognize that reason and rationality aren't at work here. Zhao Baoqing, a Chinese trade official in Washington, recently attacked the quality of U.S. goods sold in China, and pointed to cranes and to generators made by General Electric as posing serious safety hazards. Most Americans will, in this climate, probably dismiss his claims as so much empty rhetoric, but the record of safety issues with U.S.-made products should give anyone pause before doing so. . . .

A Convenient Bogeyman Instead of a Worthy Rival

China is a convenient bogeyman for all sorts of ills and fears. Without question, China presents an unparalleled challenge. At various points in the 20th century, the U.S. faced military and ideological threats. But since the dawn of the American republic, we have never faced the kind of economic challenge that China presents. It is playing the game of global capitalism almost as adeptly as we are, and our response for now seems to be a mixture of fear and disbelief.

Rather than seeing China as adding to an expanding global economic pie, we treat its ascendance as a zero-sum proposition for our workers, our companies, our currency and now even our health. While the evolution of China and the U.S. is anything but certain, and while each faces internal issues that could derail the steady move forward, one thing should be fairly clear: Our China problem is going to harm us more than it will derail China.

It is perfectly legitimate for us to demand that Chinese companies and authorities attend to product safety and to a level playing field in terms of trade. That, after all, is the guiding spirit of the World Trade Organization. It is perfectly legitimate . . . to treat China as a competitor and press the Chinese for greater access, more transparency, and assorted reforms. But much of the rhetoric and cultural undercurrent these days casts China as the on-deck enemy should al Qaeda not prove up to the task of long-term adversary.

Like it or not, China is going to be a force to contend with, just as the U.S. was a century ago. Already, we are more linked to China than most of us realize or than many would like. If China-bashing becomes the prism through which China is viewed, the recent turmoil in the markets caused by the subprime mortgage mess will seem placid by comparison.

"Hidden costs . . . suggest that outsourcing manufacturing to China is not always a simple decision."

Logistical Problems and Intellectual Property Theft Increase Costs of Outsourcing to China

Alan S. Brown

Alan S. Brown is an associate editor at the American Society of Mechanical Engineers' Mechanical Engineering magazine. His work analyzes engineering trends as well as how engineering impacts the larger economy. In the following viewpoint, Brown argues that while labor and material costs are cheaper in China, the costs associated with stolen intellectual property, complex supply chains, inflexible manufacturing schedules, and project management overhead are often unanticipated and troublesome. He remarks that businesses often spend more in overcoming these challenges than they originally expected, making the cost of offshoring much higher.

Alan S. Brown, "The China Road: The Outsourcing Option Isn't as Cheap or as Easy as It Looks," *Mechanical Engineering*, March 2005. Reproduced by permission.

As you read, consider the following questions:

1. According to Ronil Hira, what are the biggest selling exports the United States receives from China?

2. According to Chris Jones, how long did some non-Chinese companies surveyed wait for outsourced orders to reach them from China?

3. As Brown relates, what two tactics are manufacturers using to protect their intellectual property when dealing with overseas vendors?

Any discussion about how U.S. companies are outsourcing manufacturing quickly becomes a discussion about China. China's unusual combination of low wages, modern technology, and an enormous internal market of more than one billion people has forged the world's lowest-cost modern manufacturing infrastructure.

It is easy to see that labor and materials costs are cheaper in China, but it is harder to pin down the costs of stolen intellectual property, complex supply chains, inflexible manufacturing schedules, and project management overhead.

These hidden costs exist. When unmasked, they suggest that outsourcing manufacturing to China is not always a simple decision. In fact, looking for the quick bottom line fix often leads to disappointment.

Today's outsourcing is unlike waves of factory closings in the past. In the 1950s and 1960s, steel, textiles, and shipbuilding began to move overseas. In the 1970s and 1980s, consumer electronics, plastic products, and automotive parts followed.

What's different today is that some low-wage countries have begun to add technology to the mix at increasing rates. Over the past decade, the production of many advanced technology products, from circuit boards to cell phones, began to shift to such emerging Asian economies as Taiwan, Singapore, Malaysia, and South Korea. Much of that work eventually gravitated to China. By 1995, China was exporting more technology products to the United States than it was importing.

Today, says outsourcing expert Ronil Hira, an assistant professor of public policy at Rochester Institute of Technology [RIT] in New York, China's technology trickle has turned into a flood. "What are our best-selling items to China, where we ran a $2.8 billion surplus?" he asks. "Oil seeds and soybeans. What are China's biggest selling items to us? Computers, electrical machinery, and capital equipment, where Beijing ran a $50 billion surplus."

China's Economic Emergence

The emergence of China as a global market economy is an epochal event. Unlike other low-wage countries, it has a huge and growing internal market of 1.4 billion people—20 percent of the world's population—to support its factories. While vast swatches of the country are undeveloped, many areas are moving rapidly into the new century.

China's economy is huge. It has grown about 9 percent annually for the past 15 years. At $6.4 trillion, it is nearly 60 percent as large as the United States and almost twice as large as third-ranked Japan. It has become the third-largest trading nation, after the United States and Germany. Over the past decade, 120 million Chinese have moved to cities to feed its factories.

Although the average Chinese income is equivalent to only $5,000 per person, it is not distributed evenly. Along China's rapidly developing coast, income is twice the countrywide average. China's middle class, more than 100 million people strong, is larger than the entire population of Germany and somewhat smaller than that of Japan.

It has a huge appetite for consumer goods, such as cars. At five million vehicles, it is the world's third largest auto market. General Motors Corp. alone sold nearly half a million cars there in 2004. People who have visited Beijing say it has gone from a city of bicycles to a city of cars in less than five years.

Corporations from all over the world want a slice of this lucrative market. China is happy to oblige them—with one significant condition: Companies that build factories in China must transfer technology as part of the deal. Most businesses, from behemoths like GM to small firms like composite golf club maker Aldila Inc., are eager to comply.

While most of China's new factories serve the local population, many others export. More than half of all Chinese exports to the United States are from factories owned outright or partly by Taiwanese, Japanese, and U.S. companies.

China's Lax Intellectual Property Laws

The result is something new under the sun: low wages and a thriving internal market harnessed to advanced technology. Once in China, new technology tends to move freely. Chinese enforce intellectual property [IP] restrictions loosely if at all. As a result, even local Chinese companies can often compete globally.

Many are no longer competing with cheap knockoffs, low-quality goods, and labor-intensive assemblies. Instead, they are making high-definition televisions, computer displays, third-generation cell phones, and computer and networking hardware. Those high-tech products are growing faster than other Chinese exports to the United States.

Chinese original device manufacturers now engineer and manufacture everything from cell phones to PDAs [personal digital assistants] for some of the world's largest consumer electronics makers, according to Roger Wery, practice leader for outsourcing strategy at global management consulting firm Pittiglio Rabin Todd & McGrath of Mountain View, Calif. "There's not a single hour of engineering invested in these products by Palm, Sony, Ericsson, and others. They simply put their name on these cost-competitive entry-level products and engineer the more advanced models themselves."

Yet China is increasingly competitive at technology's edge. In December [2004], for example, Huawei Technologies Co. Ltd., China's largest telecommunications provider, signed a deal to build a third-generation mobile phone network to Telfort BV, the Netherlands's fifth largest mobile carrier.

"Wireless was an area where the United States and Europe were leading," Wery said. "Korea and China have closed the gap and are priced aggressively. If we don't have an IP lead on them, how long can we justify our cost advantage?"

Costs That Are Not Easy to Calculate

Low-cost labor and high-tech manufacturing have made China the leading destination for companies looking to cut costs by outsourcing production. In the past, RIT's Hira said, U.S. companies would have fought to protect domestic production.

Today, businesses embrace offshore outsourcing to cut costs. Some buy from Chinese producers. Others build their own factories or joint ventures. Even companies that want to keep manufacturing in the United States may feel forced to look offshore to remain competitive.

If China's advantages are well understood, not all of its costs are immediately obvious, according to Nicholas P. Dewhurst, executive vice president of Wakefield, R.I.-based Boothroyd Dewhurst Inc. Dewhurst works with companies that use his software to reduce manufacturing and assembly costs. Many compete or outsource to China. "I don't believe anybody yet has a handle on what outsourcing costs truly are," Dewhurst said.

"Let me give you an example," he said. "On the way to Cincinnati, I overheard someone say he had just bought a set of Callaway Golf Clubs and a bag for $250. That's a bargain because the bag alone usually goes for $350."

Reports on Revenue Losses

Intellectual property risks are among the top three operating issues currently facing multinational companies with operations in China, according to a survey by a committee of the Beijing-based China Association of Enterprises With Foreign Investment, a coalition of multinational companies that have invested more than $60 billion in China. About 10% of surveyed members estimated revenue losses due to intellectual property violations of more than 20%.

Gloria Gonzalez,
"Top Risk in China? Intellectual Property Theft,"
Financial Week, *August 13, 2007.*

"There was a problem, and he sent them back to Callaway for repair," Dewhurst said. "Callaway wouldn't touch it. It was a Chinese knockoff, copied right down to the patent numbers. How do you, as Callaway, capture the cost of that?"

Although Callaway was not able to verify this specific incident, a spokesman said the company would not repair counterfeit articles. According to a press release issued early ... [in 2004,] Callaway pursued enforcement actions in 11 countries in 2003. The actions involved 37,000 individual counterfeit products, including golf clubs, clothes, and bags. The company said one case, which resulted in a criminal charge against a U.S. reseller, was traced back to a supplier in China.

The cost of stolen intellectual property and lost opportunities is not as easy to calculate as the cost of labor when deciding whether or not to outsource. Many companies also underestimate the time and energy needed to manage projects on the other side of the globe or to master the complex supply chain from China.

Lengthy Supply Chains

Few hard numbers about the true cost of doing business in China are readily available. Recently, however, firms such as Pittiglio Rabin Todd & McGrath and supply chain consultant Aberdeen Group Inc. of Boston have conducted studies that are examining some of these issues.

The 7,000-mile supply chain that stretches from China to the United States is the most obvious place to dig for hidden costs.

"Logistics costs in the United States are below 3 percent of revenue," according to Aberdeen's senior vice president of research, Chris Jones. "Our study found companies in China were paying from 6 to 12 percent of revenue, depending on product and factory location."

"People sometimes don't understand all the complexity involved when going from truck-based shipping in a single country to cross-border, multimode logistics," Jones said. "We're talking about goods passing through the hands of 17 to 24 different parties. They include manufacturers, crate forwarders, consolidators, customs and regulatory agencies, carriers, ports, and more."

It is easy to underestimate potential revenue losses when bringing products into the United States. Last holiday season, for example, companies struggled to bring goods to market by Christmas. For some, port backups made the difference between full price or profit-eating markdowns.

Jones found that 42 percent of the firms he studied took more than 60 days to receive an order from China, compared with only two weeks in the United States. Surprisingly, 89 percent of the firms with the longest lead times also had the highest logistics costs.

"You'd think slow shipments would be cheap, but it indicates that they don't know how to run their supply chain," Jones said. "They are the ones paying extra for expedited shipping or writing off their Christmas revenue."

Wery at Pittiglio Rabin Todd & McGrath agrees. Companies frequently spend more on air shipments than planned. This makes up for inflexible supply chains that have four to five weeks of products in transit at any given time. Importers often tie up extra money in inventory to guard against shortages.

Slow Reaction to Schedule Changes

Extented supply chains are also slow to react to schedule changes, Wery said. "A producer in the United States can respond within 24 hours to changes in product mix, such as color, packaging, and delivery location," he said. "In Mexico, it takes about three or four days. In China, they need five to six weeks."

That creates huge problems for companies in markets where new looks and features count. "If you're six months behind the market leader, your revenue potential could be cut in half," Wery said. "On paper, outsourcing saves money, but your time to market is not guaranteed.

"Right now, we're working with a client that is doing systems engineering in California, writing software in Russia, and manufacturing the electronics in Malaysia. All the back-and-forth between different time zones impacts time to market. They might have been better off spending 20 to 30 percent more for the product and getting to market earlier."

Because the supply chain is so long and rigid, most successful practitioners limit outsourcing to products or standard components that rarely require changes and have established, predictable markets. Others prefer near-shoring in places like Mexico, where they save on labor but can respond faster to market fluctuations.

Dividing Product Manufacturing Among Vendors

Intellectual property is a major concern for anyone who does business in China. The Callaway golf clubs are only flotsam in a flood of knockoffs that deluge the United States each year.

"IP is an issue in China and in the Asia Pacific region, and it's nothing we should be shy about," said Kevin Elgood, engineering director for TRW Automotive Holdings Corp.'s Asia Pacific Technology Center in Shanghai, China. "They do reverse engineering and they have little regard for IP."

One of the reasons TRW established its own engineering center in China was to give the company more control over its own and customers' intellectual property. Even so, advanced technology development remains in the United States; Chinese engineers adapt the designs to local markets.

This helps, but it is no sure solution, according to Wery. "If you have engineers offshore, they become prime targets for Chinese companies seeking to hire talent," he said. "Poaching happens, so you're never completely protected."

Companies have other ways to protect themselves. They slice projects into modules, retaining value added systems engineering at home, while outsourcing mechanical engineering, electrical engineering, and manufacturing to different vendors. This keeps any one company from reverse engineering an entire product.

Other companies send out only low-value work. "Take tools and dies, for example," said automotive analyst David Cole, chairman of the Center for Automotive Research in Ann Arbor, Mich. "You can do the rough cut anywhere in the world. You just pick who has the lowest price. It's the sophisticated fitting of the dies in the plant that adds value, and you have to be on the scene to do that."

Developed nations continue to pressure China to fully enforce patents and other intellectual property protection. Some companies have hired investigators to collect evidence. Even when China shuts down violators, many simply relocate elsewhere. . . .

The Gap in Project Management

Many firms are unprepared for the amount of project management—including late-night phone calls, last-minute travel, and supply chain monitoring—needed to bring an outsourcing relationship up to speed. It may take months or even years of heavy travel to ensure that both parties understand one another. Even then, companies need strong, consistent internal processes to avoid problems.

Sometimes, Chinese companies cut corners to meet price expectations of foreign customers. "Those businesses are often very entrepreneurial and not very mature," Wery said. "They do not have established processes, infrastructure, training, or management. To achieve cost targets, they need to cut corners and end up doing things you would never do in the U.S., especially in environmental areas."

Some Western firms look the other way. Others cannot afford to. They remember how low labor costs led to consumer boycotts against companies like Nike and Ikea during the 1990s. They worry about consumer reaction to charges of military-enforced labor or toxic disasters. Still, said Wery, it is an uphill battle to impose key metrics beyond those relating to cost.

China's combination of low labor costs and modern technology—aided by lax intellectual property enforcement—makes it a manufacturing powerhouse. Its increasingly prosperous internal market enables efficiencies of scale. . . .

Creating a Collaborative Business Model

It takes time and commitment to make Chinese manufacturing relationships work. In some cases, they may not work at all. As companies learn the hidden costs of outsourcing, they may find it does not yield the promised savings. This is especially true for products that require customization, proprietary technology, or quicker reaction to market trends.

Auto analyst Cole predicts that the flexible U.S. economy will adjust to China just as it adjusted to Japan during the 1970s and 1980s.

"When we studied how Chinese manufacturing impacted the auto industry in Michigan, we first saw China as a competitor," he said. "But you can't go head-to-head with China due to labor costs. Instead, we're now looking at China as a partner."

"The auto industry is in the middle of adopting a new business model that involves collaborating in real time across nontraditional boundaries," Cole said. "This creates threats and opportunities. The threat is that they will come after our markets. The opportunity is that China's new wealth will create a middle class market for us."

That is, of course, classic economics: Every country benefits from free trade. But that doesn't mean every industry and every business will benefit. The struggle of manufacturers to bounce back from the latest recession may be proof that a shakeout is in the works.

It is far from clear who the winners and losers will be.

> *"Despite its drawbacks, ... the call-center boom is widely considered a blessing to the economy."*

Outsourcing Is Transforming Life in the Philippines

Audrey Carpio

In the following viewpoint, Audrey Carpio claims that the Philippines is an emerging outsourcing destination for information technology (IT) industries. Growth is especially apparent in the call center sector, which is expected to employ more than a million Filipinos by 2010, Carpio explains. With this burgeoning workforce, the economy and the culture of the nation are changing, Carpio asserts. Audrey Carpio is a display copy chief for New York Review of Magazines. *She formerly worked at a Filipino newspaper.*

As you read, consider the following questions:

1. According to Carpio, what gives the Philippines definite advantages over India as an outsourcing destination?

2. Why is not everyone fit to work in the emerging IT industry in the Philippines, as Carpio relates?

3. As Carpio explains, why is an English-speaking policy enforced in all aspects of call center life?

It is called the country's latest sunshine industry, but thousands of call-center employees in the Philippines barely get to see the light of day. As dusk settles and most others are heading home, customer-support representatives begin their nocturnal shifts, energized by take-out food from the nearby McDonald's or Starbucks franchises located in the shadow of Business Process Outsourcing buildings, or BPOs. These boxy new edifices, taking their place along the skyline of Manila's financial district, Makati, are emblazoned with high-tech names like ePerformax, eTelecare, and InnovaQuest.

Call-center employees have to adjust to a new sleep cycle as well as a new way of speaking, sometimes even a new name—answering callers from America and Britain, who ask technical questions about their recently purchased computer, such as, "Why is the cup holder not working?" (Answer: "Because it's a CD-ROM drive.")

Yet new graduates are flocking to the industry, and it's not hard to see why: The average starting salary of $275 a month is well above minimum wage of about $6 a day.

"Call centers have modern workplaces, offer good wages, and you are likely to be surrounded by young people. The job usually attracts people aged 19–35 years old, regardless of their course in college," an operations supervisor at Advanced Contact Solutions, Hazel Manzano, 26, explained.

An exception to the age norm is Linda Cahilig, who, at 52, occupies an entry-level position as a customer-care representative at a top BPO. But because of her extensive previous experience at traditional companies and her two master's degrees, she is also a communications coach, with long-term goals of contributing in the training department. Her reasons for joining, just six months ago, were idealistic; she is hopeful for what the industry can do for the Philippines. "I like the fact that it is currently employing a lot of our graduates. Dedicated people who work well but would most likely be mismatched with the job requirements in traditional companies . . . are the very ones attracted to the call centers. Personally, I want to do something to make our country the top BPO country in the world."

An Emerging Global Competitor

The Philippines, which has 105,000 of its citizens employed in the call-center industry, is quickly catching up to India, which has 270,000, according to the 2006 Asian Contact Center Industry Benchmarking Report.

The Philippine government is predicting that the country's high growth rate will result in more than a million Filipinos working as customer-service representatives by 2010. With a large population of English speakers (English is one of the country's official languages), a strong cultural affinity with America, lower unit costs, and lower attrition rates, the Philippines has definite advantages over India.

But to make the Philippines even more competitive, President [Gloria Macapagal-]Arroyo . . . announced [in May 2006] the release of $10 million for "call-center finishing schools," or training programs intended to improve the English skills of Filipinos.

Culture Clashes

Betraying one's whereabouts with an accent accident can change the course of a simple conversation. "American customers don't care if you're Indian or Filipino. As long as you're not American and have a strong accent, you are likely to get racially abused by some callers. Sometimes at the start of the call, they will ask, 'Where are you located?' and will request for an American representative right away," Ms. Manzano said.

Telephone agents are often on the receiving end of American customers' aggression, as many American jobs continue to

The Philippines Focus on Human Capital

Cabinet Secretary [L. Ricardo] Saludo says the government is focused on developing human capital through education and training to keep a steady supply of talent for the outsourcing sector. Manila is also beefing up the telecommunications infrastructure, he says.

Chasing the outsourcing wave is a smart strategy for an economy such as the Philippines' [economy]. Compared with capital-intensive manufacturing, service businesses are cheap to set up, and can generate a hundred times more jobs per dollar invested. President [Gloria Macapagal-]Arroyo recently earmarked $10 million for new trainees in the outsourcing industry. Students interested in outsourcing jobs are given vouchers that can be used for tuition at vocational institutes.

Assif Shameen,
"The Philippines' Awesome Outsourcing Opportunity,"
Business Week, September 19, 2006.

float offshore. Valerie De Leon, 30, said she got her most difficult calls when she handled Dell Customer Care. "Imagine this—a customer asks for a full refund for a computer that's already two years old." Ms. De Leon naturally denied the request and was then subjected to name-calling and cursing. Doing callbacks once, she was greeted with this message on the answering machine: "If you're some moron telemarketer from India or the Philippines, back off and don't you leave any messages, you . . . freaks!" Now that she works with eBay's British branch to restore account takeovers by hackers, she doesn't do phone calls anymore, but she is still required to use a Western-sounding alias in her e-mails. "This is to avoid cultural discrimination. Even if I have an English-sounding first name, I wouldn't want to use it and end up being abused by irate customers."

Ms. De Leon gets annoyed when people think customer-service agents merely take in calls, like telephone operators. "Customer care is the 'whining end,' so I'm not surprised when some of my colleagues would resign in just three days after we hit the floor," she said. "Not everyone is psychologically fit to work in call centers." The abuse from callers and the abnormal hours—a shift may start at 7 p.m. and end at 10 a.m.—take their toll on the agents' health, too. Nicotine- and caffeine-addiction as well as eye, ear, and throat disorders are many of the growing concerns of representatives and their employers. Ms. De Leon has spent two Christmases and a New Year's at the office, and she has gotten sick several times. Her work schedule forces Ms. Manzano, who has an infant, to sacrifice time she would otherwise spend with her child. "The baby sleeps with my parents at night. Sometimes, I just have to use my sick leaves when there is no one to take care of the baby."

The environment and its regulations can also be a psychological strain. For instance, an English-speaking policy is enforced at all call centers, not only on the floor but also in pantries and elevators, mostly to maintain a seamless sense of temporality and location for the American callers. "In reality, people don't follow this rule," Ms. Manzano added. "Filipinos love to talk and are more comfortable using their language."

Creating a New Culture

Ms. Manzano, who's been working for BPOs since she graduated from college, started a comic strip about call-center life. "'Callwork . . .' pays tribute to the BPO workforce in the Philippines." Written in Taglish, the lingua franca of the Philippine people and press, the comic pokes gentle fun at call-center life. First published in her company's quarterly magazine, Ms. Manzano now relishes national exposure in the *Manila Bulletin*, keeping true to the spirit of the call-center employee: an identity-disoriented, highly caffeinated night owl, an affecter of twangs and stateside slang, and a locator of lost dial tones.

In one strip, the first panel begins with a caller asking a representative, "Where am I calling?"

The agent answers, "Philippines, ma'am." And the caller then responds with anguish, "Oh my gosh!!! I'm calling long distance! I must hang up!"

Despite its drawbacks, however, the call-center boom is widely considered a blessing to the economy.

Mau Perez, 26, who is a trainer at Teleperformance for a mobile phone company account, said: "A cab driver once told me that hc thanks call centers for the increase in passengers at night—just three years ago, the streets were dull and lifeless."

Now, there's enough traffic for fast-food joints to remain open 24 hours, and thousands more nocturnal Filipinos are fueling up on energy drinks and lattés, keeping the night abuzz.

Periodical Bibliography

The following articles have been selected to supplement the diverse views presented in this chapter.

Frederik Balfour   "Vietnam's Growing Role in Outsourcing," *Business Week*, December 11, 2006.

Anand Giridharadas   "India's Edge Goes Beyond Outsourcing," *New York Times*, April 4, 2007.

S. Mitra Kalita   "India's New Faces of Outsourcing," *Washington Post*, January 11, 2006.

Rachael King   "Outsourcing: Beyond Bangalore," *Business Week*, December 11, 2006.

Rama Lakshmi   "U.S. Legal Work Booms in India," *Washington Post*, May 11, 2008.

Don Lee   "China Marches into Outsourcing," *Los Angeles Times*, April 8, 2008.

Alvaro Vargas Llosa   "Eight Myths About India," *Independent Review*, February 2, 2006.

Assif Shameen   "The Philippines' Awesome Outsourcing Opportunity," *Business Week*, September 19, 2006.

Amol Sharma,   "In India, Parents Become Part of the Hiring
Jackie Range, and   Picture," *Wall Street Journal*, May 27, 2008.
Vibhuti Agarwal

Noem Sheiber   "News and Analysis; As a Center for Outsourcing, India Could Be Losing Its Edge," *New York Times*, May 9, 2004.

Bill Steigerwald   "India Rising," *Human Events*, April 10, 2007.

Vivek Wadhwa   "India's Workforce Revolution," *Wall Street Journal*, July 23, 2008.

For Further Discussion

Chapter 1

1. The discussion over the impact of outsourcing can be emotionally charged when it comes to the topic of potential American job losses. Keeping this in mind, how does Steven Greenhouse's use of one individual's experience influence your feelings about outsourcing? Why do you think Greenhouse chooses to include this narrative in his viewpoint? On the other hand, Brink Lindsey sticks mostly to statistics and research studies in his viewpoint when arguing that outsourcing will not harm American workers or take away jobs. Do you find this tactic more or less convincing than Greenhouse's? Which author do you feel makes the better argument either for or against outsourcing as it relates to American workers, and why?

2. Daniel T. Griswold and Dale D. Buss argue that outsourcing is one way to ensure that U.S. businesses remain competitive on a global scale and ultimately benefit the American people. L. Josh Bivens opposes this notion, stating that many studies reporting the benefits of outsourcing to the U.S. economy have assumed too much and wrongly generalized the benefits to individual corporations as being indicative of benefits on a national scale. Conduct some further research into the costs of consumer products in America. Are consumers in the United States paying less for goods today than they were previously, as many proponents of outsourcing state? Is the quality of these goods higher than it has been previously? Based on your findings, do you feel that outsourcing has benefited the American economy and people?

3. Proponents of outsourcing often claim that building plants and employing workers in foreign countries is not a new trend. They contend, as does Milton Ezrati, that throughout America's recent history, critics have raised concerns over foreign workforces stealing jobs from U.S. workers, yet these claims have eventually proved inconsequential. However, economist Alan S. Blinder argues that while previous outsourcing mainly involved manufacturing jobs, the current wave of outsourcing has resulted in the loss of jobs for many white-collar workers, which would make the consequences of current outsourcing practices different than those experienced in the past. Based on the viewpoints in this chapter, does outsourcing seem different today than in the past? Can the examples of the past be applied to outsourcing today? Support your ideas with evidence from each of the viewpoints in this chapter.

Chapter 2

1. Critics of military outsourcing claim that there are certain tasks that can be performed only by the government, tasks that are "inherently governmental." Peter W. Singer argues along these lines, presenting some of the problems with allowing private companies to perform jobs that were previously performed only by government entities. However, proponents, such as Doug Brooks and Matan Chorev, maintain that private military firms greatly benefit the military and the United States as a whole by reducing costs and playing an important supporting role. After reviewing these two viewpoints, whose argument do you find more convincing? Do you believe that there are certain government responsibilities that should not be handed over to private companies? Explain your answer, citing from the viewpoints.

2. Following the September 11, 2001, terrorist attacks against the World Trade Center and the Pentagon, some have called for a restructuring of agencies, such as the Federal Bureau of Investigations (FBI) and Central Intelligence Agency (CIA), to ensure that no further attacks are carried out against the United States. Michael Rubin argues that restructuring is not sufficient. Instead, he contends that privatization of the CIA would encourage competition, create a higher quality agent, and remove bureaucratic barriers stifling the intelligence collection process. Tim Shorrock disagrees and worries that privatization would create more secrecy and reduce accountability to the public. Based on what you know about national security, do you feel that outsourcing intelligence jobs to private companies would improve federal agencies' abilities to fight terrorism? Explain your answer.

3. Since the September 11, 2001, terrorist attacks, much of the national security debate has centered on how terrorists enter the country and the ways in which they could smuggle deadly materials across national borders. While many argue that a country in the Middle East, such as the United Arab Emirates (UAE), should not handle U.S. port security, James K. Glassman maintains that since the terrorist attacks, the UAE has had an exemplary record fighting terrorism and that denying a Muslim nation that is friendly to the United States could decrease national security. Do you believe that the country where a company is based impacts how it conducts business? After reading the viewpoint by Michael E. O'Hanlon, would your view change if that company is engaged in a business that could impact the nation's security?

Chapter 3

1. Ron Hira and William H. Gates take opposite sides in the debate over guest worker visas in the technology fields.

Hira contends that America needs to invest in its own workers and keep its technical force well skilled to compete in the global marketplace. Gates, on the other hand, maintains that America does not produce enough skilled technicians and that without large numbers of guest workers American companies will lose their edge in the global market. Citing examples from the arguments of both authors, explain what impact you think the limiting or expanding of guest worker visas would have on America's ability to compete globally.

2. After reading the viewpoint by Shannon Klinger and M. Lynn Sykes and the one by Russ Feingold, explain how you would regulate the federal government's consumption of foreign goods and services. Do you believe the government should always look first to U.S. suppliers and contractors, or should the government be free to weigh cost and availability before buying American? Be sure to defend your answer against critics who would champion the opposite view.

Chapter 4

1. Do you believe, as Zachary Karabell contends, that Americans have a fear of China based on a belief that China produces shoddy, sometimes dangerous, goods? How does Karabell explain this fear? Do you agree with his assessment? Explain why or why not. Do you believe America might fear India in the same way?

2. Alan S. Brown notes that offshoring has its price. In the case of China, Brown suggests that fears of intellectual property theft and logistical problems keep some businesses from outsourcing and leave others with trade agreements that end up costing more than expected. Do some research on these problems and explain what, if anything, is being done to remedy them.

3. Audrey Carpio reveals how outsourced jobs are transforming life and culture in the Philippines. Do further research and find out how outsourcing is affecting other countries, such as India. In an essay, explain what changes are taking place in these countries and decide if you think these transformations are positive or negative.

Organizations to Contact

The editors have compiled the following list of organizations concerned with the issues debated in this book. The descriptions are derived from materials provided by the organizations. All have publications or information available for interested readers. The list was compiled on the date of publication of the present volume; the information provided here may change. Be aware that many organizations take several weeks or longer to respond to inquiries, so allow as much time as possible.

American Enterprise Institute (AEI)
1150 Seventeenth Street NW, Washington, DC   20036
(202) 862-5800 • fax: (202) 862-7177
Web site: www.aei.org

Founded in 1943, the American Enterprise Institute (AEI) works to promote conservative public policy that exemplifies the ideals of limited government, private enterprise, individual liberty and responsibility, and vigilant and effective defense and foreign policy. As such, many of the publications and reports by AEI scholars extol the benefits of outsourcing to the American economy. Additionally, the organization advocates a non-protectionist approach to address both economic and national security concerns. *The American* is the bimonthly magazine of AEI and contains articles concerning topics such as outsourcing and U.S. national security.

**American Federation of Labor and Congress
of Industrial Organizations (AFL-CIO)**
815 Sixteenth Street NW, Washington, DC   20006
Web site: www.afl-cio.org

The American Federation of Labor and Congress of Industrial Organizations (AFL-CIO) is a voluntary membership organization for national and international labor unions representing workers in professions varying from teachers to truck drivers, musicians to miners, and firefighters to farm workers, to name a few. The organization is dedicated to improving the lives of working families by ensuring economic justice in the workplace and social justice nationwide. The AFL-CIO believes that building a labor movement where workers have a voice in policy decisions will best preserve these workers' rights. The organization's Web site offers fact sheets, reports, transcripts of testimony, and other informative documents concerning the impact of outsourcing on the American worker and suggesting policy that benefits workers.

Cato Institute
1000 Massachusetts Avenue NW
Washington, DC   20001-5403
(202) 842-0200 • fax: (202) 842-3490
Web site: www.cato.org

The Cato Institute is a think tank seeking to advance public policies that coincide with Libertarian values and principles such as belief in a free market economic system and limited government intervention into the private lives of American citizens. Cato contends that outsourcing strengthens the American economy in the long run, resulting in the creation of new jobs for U.S. citizens, but questions the outsourcing of military and intelligence duties to private contractors. Periodic publications of the institute include the tri-annual *Cato Journal* and the quarterly *Cato's Letters*. The organization's Web site offers additional articles covering issues relating to outsourcing.

Communications Workers of America (CWA)
501 Third Street NW, Washington, DC   20001
(202) 434-1100 • fax: (202) 434-1279
e-mail: cwaweb@cwa-union.org
Web site: www.cwa-union.org

Communications Workers of America (CWA) is a national labor union representing individuals working in telecommunications, broadcasting, cable TV, journalism, publishing, and other communications and customer service fields. The union works to organize and facilitate community and political action to ensure that corporations running the communications industry observe and fulfill the rights and needs of members. One project of the CWA is the OutsourceOutrage.com Web site, which provides information about individuals whose jobs have been outsourced to other countries and offers individuals an opportunity to join campaigns to combat the continual offshoring of U.S. jobs. Additional information about outsourcing issues can be obtained on the CWA Web site.

CorpWatch
1611 Telegraph Avenue, #720, Oakland, CA   94612
(510) 271-8080
Web site: www.corpwatch.org

The mission of CorpWatch is to hold corporations accountable for their actions, ensure that human rights are observed worldwide, and to expose environmental crimes, fraud, and corruption. The organization has kept close watch on the companies receiving government contracts related to the wars on terror and in Iraq and Afghanistan. Additionally, CorpWatch founded the Web site Warprofiteers.com to provide information specifically about the outsourcing of military duties to private companies. CorpWatch has also chronicled and researched the impact of offshoring on American workers. Copies of CorpWatch reports can be read and downloaded from the organization's Web site.

Council on Foreign Relations (CFR)
The Harold Pratt House, 58 E. Sixty-Eighth Street
New York, NY   10065
(212) 434-9400 • fax: (212) 434-9800
Web site: www.cfr.org

The Council on Foreign Relations (CFR) is a nonpartisan, membership think tank seeking to provide educational information on government foreign policy to its members, government officials, the media, the public, and any individual interested in learning about the processes and outcomes of foreign policy making. While the council takes no institutional position on foreign policy decisions, it does provide a forum for a diverse collection of scholars to debate their positions and provide a broad view of policy choices. CFR has published numerous articles concerning outsourcing and its relationship to U.S. trade policy in general, as well as outsourcing with regard to the U.S. military. Many articles can be found in *Foreign Affairs*, the bimonthly journal of the CFR.

Economic Policy Institute (EPI)
1333 H Street NW, Suite 300, East Tower
Washington, DC   20005-4707
(202) 775-8810 • fax: (202) 775-0819
e-mail: epi@epi.org
Web site: www.epi.org

The Economic Policy Institute (EPI) seeks to achieve a prosperous and fair economy in the United States by facilitating public debate about what strategies would be most beneficial in achieving this goal. Thus, the institute attempts to educate citizens so that they have the ability to make informed decisions that will impact economic policy making. It also believes that a strong labor movement is essential to ensuring that the conditions of working people in the United States are improved. EPI offers a comprehensive issue guide concerning offshoring as well as a list of links to online resources and other print resources. The *EPI Journal* is the official publication of the institute.

GlobalSecurity.org
300 N. Washington Street, Suite B-100
Alexandria, VA   22314
(703) 548-2700 • fax: (703) 548-2424
e-mail: info@globalsecurity.org
Web site: www.globalsecurity.org

GlobalSecurity.org serves as an Internet clearinghouse of information concerning topics relating to the military, weapons of mass destruction, intelligence, homeland security, and security-related topics. The Web site offers individuals a searchable database of articles, with many articles discussing the use of private military companies and government contracting for intelligence and military duties. Additionally, globalsecurity.org provides free, downloadable white papers covering security topics and a list of security-related magazines offering free subscriptions.

Heritage Foundation
214 Massachusetts Avenue NE, Washington, DC 20002-4999
(202) 546-4400 • fax: (202) 546-8328
e-mail: info@heritage.org
Web site: www.heritage.org

The Heritage Foundation is a conservative public policy institute dedicated to the promotion of policies consistent with the ideas of free enterprise, limited government, individual freedom, traditional American values, and a strong national defense. In accordance with these principles, the foundation supports companies' right to outsource jobs, arguing that outsourcing benefits both the corporations and the consumers, resulting in greater productivity, improved living standards for Americans, and more jobs in the United States. The Heritage Foundation's webmemos and backgrounders outlining the organization's stance on outsourcing and related issues can be read on its Web site.

International Peace Operations Association (IPOA)
1900 L Street NW, Washington, DC 20036
(202) 464-0721 • fax: (202) 464-0726
Web site: www.ipoaonline.org

The International Peace Operations Association (IPOA) believes that the private sector could play a large and helpful role in securing nations riddled with conflict worldwide. In accordance, this organization serves as a trade association for the private Peace and Stability Industry, promoting best operations and ethics practices, consulting with policy makers as to what regulations are appropriate for the industry, and educating the public about the role the industry plays in peace-keeping and military operations. IPOA views military outsourcing as essential in today's demilitarized world. The *Journal of the International Peace Operations* (*JIPO*) is the official publication of the organization; many articles from the journal can be read on the IPOA's Web site.

National Bureau of Economic Research (NBER)

1050 Massachusetts Avenue, Cambridge, MA   02138-5398
(617) 868-3900 • fax: (617) 868-2742
Web site: www.nber.org

The National Bureau of Economic Research (NBER) seeks to promote a more complete understanding of the workings of the United States economy by conducting and publishing research for policy makers, business professionals, and scholars. Numerous reports addressing the issue of outsourcing and its impact on the U.S. economy can be read online in addition to complete issues of the *NBER Digest*.

Peterson Institute

1750 Massachusetts Avenue NW
Washington, DC   20036-1903
(202) 328-9000 • fax: (202) 659-3225
e-mail: comments@petersoninstitute.org
Web site: www.petersoninstitute.org

The Peterson Institute is dedicated to providing nonpartisan research on international economic policy and is widely recognized for its neutral viewpoints. With regard to outsourcing, the organization's reports often examine both the pros and cons of outsourcing, looking at its impact on both individuals and corporations, as well as the American economy at large. Copies of these reports, as well as other commentaries and policy briefs can be obtained on the Peterson Institute Web site.

Progressive Policy Institute (PPI)

600 Pennsylvania Avenue SE, Suite 400

Washington, DC 20003

(202) 547-0001 • fax: (202) 544-5014

Web site: www.ppionline.org

The Progressive Policy Institute (PPI) offers a progressive perspective on how government policy should serve the citizens of the United States, moving away from traditional views and the left-right debate and insisting that the government should serve its citizens and the needs of their communities. Additionally, the institute advocates for policies that strengthen international and political freedom. PPI publications highlight the benefits of outsourcing on both Americans and individuals worldwide. PPI scholars question the value of outsourcing government jobs to the private sector. On the PPI Web site, interested individuals can subscribe to periodic e-newsletters as well as read press releases, op-eds, and other PPI publications.

Reason Foundation

3415 S. Sepulveda Boulevard, Suite 400

Los Angeles, CA 90034

(310) 391-2245 • fax: (310) 391-4395

Web site: www.reason.org

The Reason Foundation has been supporting policies in accordance with the libertarian principles of individual liberty, free markets, and the rule of law, since its founding in 1968. Reports covering the topic of outsourcing focus on the benefits this business practice provides for American corporations and workers, including increased productivity, insourcing of jobs, and better value for consumers. The official magazine of the organization, *Reason*, and the bimonthly journal, *Privatization Watch*, both cover topics relating to outsourcing as well as general trade issues.

United States Government Accountability Office (GAO)
414 G Street NW, Washington, DC 20548
(202) 512-3000
e-mail: contact@gao.gov
Web site: www.gao.gov

The United States Government Accountability Office (GAO), often referred to as the "congressional watchdog," is a nonpartisan, independent agency of the United States government charged with ensuring that the federal government is working to the benefit of the American people. GAO will investigate issues or concerns of congressional committees or subcommittees on request. The organization has testified before Congress and produced reports concerning many facets of outsourcing and its impact on America, with regard to issues such as security and economics. The GAO Web site offers a searchable collection of these reports and testimonies.

Bibliography of Books

Deborah D. Avant   *The Market for Force: The Consequences of Privatizing Security.* New York: Cambridge University Press, 2005.

Todd G. Buchholz   *Bringing the Jobs Home: How the Left Created the Outsourcing Crisis—and How We Can Fix It.* New York: Sentinel, 2004.

Jack Buffington   *An Easy Out: Corporate America's Addiction to Outsourcing.* Westport, CT: Praeger, 2007.

Nicholas C. Burkholder   *Outsourcing: The Definitive View, Applications and Implications.* Hoboken, NJ: Wiley, 2006.

Erran Carmel and Paul Tjia   *Offshoring Information Technology: Sourcing and Outsourcing to a Global Workforce.* New York: Cambridge University Press, 2005.

Michael F. Corbett   *The Outsourcing Revolution: Why It Makes Sense and How to Do It Right.* Chicago, IL: Dearborn Trade, 2004.

Paul Davies   *What's This India Business?: Offshoring, Outsourcing, and the Global Services Revolution.* Yarmouth, ME: Nicholas Brealey International, 2004.

Lou Dobbs — *Exporting America: Why Corporate Greed Is Shipping American Jobs Overseas*. New York: Warner Business Books, 2004.

Lou Dobbs — *War on the Middle Class: How the Government, Big Business, and Special Interest Groups Are Waging War on the American Dream and How to Fight Back*. New York: Viking, 2006.

Byron L. Dorgan — *Take This Job and Ship It: How Corporate Greed and Brain-Dead Politics Are Selling Out America*. New York: Thomas Dunne Books, 2006.

Peter Engardio, ed. — *Chindia: How China and India Are Revolutionizing Global Business*. New York: McGraw Hill, 2007.

Christopher M. England — *Outsourcing the American Dream: Pain and Pleasure in the Era of Downsizing*. Lincoln, NE: Writers Club Press, 2001.

Diana Farrell, ed. — *Offshoring: Understanding the Emerging Global Labor Market*. Boston, MA: Harvard Business School Press, 2006.

Ron French — *Driven Abroad: The Outsourcing of America*. Muskegon, MI: RDR Books, 2006.

Steve Hamm — *Bangalore Tiger: How Indian Tech Upstart Wipro Is Rewriting the Rules of Global Competition*. New York: McGraw Hill, 2007.

Ann E. Harrison and Margaret S. McMillan	*Outsourcing Jobs?: Multinationals and U.S. Employment.* Cambridge, MA: National Bureau of Economic Research, 2006.
Ron Hira and Anil Hira	*Outsourcing America: What's Behind Our National Crisis and How We Can Reclaim American Jobs.* New York: American Management Association, 2005.
Harbhajan Kehal and Varinder P. Singh, eds.	*Outsourcing and Offshoring in the 21st Century: A Socio-Economic Perspective.* Hershey, PA: Idea Group, 2006.
Mark Kobayashi-Hillary	*Outsourcing to India: The Offshore Advantage.* New York: Springer, 2004.
Thomas M. Koulopoulos and Tom Roloff	*Smartsourcing: Driving Innovation and Growth Through Outsourcing.* Avon, MA: Platinum Press, 2006.
Runjuan Liu and Daniel Trefler	*Much Ado About Nothing: American Jobs and the Rise of Service Outsourcing to China and India.* Cambridge, MA: National Bureau of Economic Research, 2008.
N. Gregory Mankiw and Phillip Swagel	*The Politics and Economics of Offshore Outsourcing.* Cambridge, MA: National Bureau of Economic Research, 2006.
Robyn Meredith	*The Elephant and the Dragon: The Rise of India and China and What It Means for All of Us.* New York: W.W. Norton, 2007.

Robert Young Pelton — *Licensed to Kill: Hired Guns in the War on Terror*. New York: Crown, 2006.

Vinay Rai and William L. Simon — *Think India: The Rise of the World's Next Superpower and What It Means for Every American*. New York: Dutton, 2007.

Jeremy Scahill — *Blackwater: The Rise of the World's Most Powerful Mercenary Army*. New York: Nation Books, 2007.

Oded Shenkar — *The Chinese Century: The Rising Chinese Economy and Its Impact on the Global Economy, the Balance of Power, and Your Job*. Upper Saddle River, NJ: Wharton School Publishing, 2005.

Tim Shorrock — *Spies for Hire: The Secret World of Intelligence Outsourcing*. New York: Simon & Schuster, 2008.

P.W. Singer — *Corporate Warriors: The Rise of the Privatized Military Industry*. Ithaca, NY: Cornell University Press, 2003.

Joseph E. Stiglitz — *Making Globalization Work*. New York: W.W. Norton, 2006.

Alan Tonelson — *The Race to the Bottom: Why a Worldwide Worker Surplus and Uncontrolled Free Trade Are Sinking American Living Standards*. Cambridge, MA: Westview, 2000.

Atul Vashistha and Avinash Vashistha   *The Offshore Nation: Strategies for Success in Global Outsourcing and Offshoring.* New York: Tata McGraw-Hill, 2006.

Paul R. Verkuil   *Outsourcing Sovereignty: Why Privatization of Government Functions Threatens Democracy and What We Can Do About It.* New York: Cambridge University Press, 2007.

Index